The essential guide to
festivals

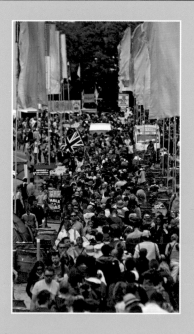

Sharon Watson

Contents

TENTS AND MUD AND ROCK 'N' ROLL

What is a festival?

Daft question, surely? Absolutely not. When once every village boasted a fête or fair, these days the buzz word is festival. For the purposes of this guide, we've had to apply some strict definitions.

First, it must be more than a one-day event. You do get one-day festivals – often in city parks – but face it, unless you are there long enough to HAVE to use the toilets, you are missing out on an essential festival experience. We do cover one-day events in the 'festivals lite' section (see pages 74–75).

Second, it has to be on a self-contained site. Usually this means camping. Sometimes, in rare and special cases, it means a bunch of music fans of one type or another taking over a holiday camp for a weekend. So, loosely themed events, such as the Camden Crawl, that take place across a bunch of neighbourhood venues, while everyday life goes on all around, don't make the cut in this book.

Third, music has to be a main focus of the festival. So that rules out vehicle owners' club rallies like Vanfest, literary festivals, as well as skate and surf festivals – although most have great line-ups of music as part of the entertainment.

Fourth and finally, it should really be a repeating event. With an explosion in new festival launches over the last couple of summers, not all will make it. We have to be fairly sure that any festivals featured here will still be around in a year's time.

That said, we can tweak our own rules if we think it will make the guide more readable, more entertaining and more useful – or to highlight a special or particular event that really deserves a mention!

Background

Forty years after the summer evening when Jefferson Airplane brought
San Francisco psychedelia to the Isle of Wight, the festival culture launched
then is enjoying a new golden age.

   Three generations of British youth have contributed to our festival
heritage. Originally seeded by the sixties hippy movement, it was tended
and grown by seventies rockers. It was almost killed off by eighties
anarchists and their arch-enemies, the state, but enjoyed a growth spurt
among the grunge and Britpop generation of the nineties. Now, in 2008, its
roots are firmly embedded at the heart of British popular culture and the
branches of the festival heritage spread far and wide.

   Back in the sixties, a simpler time made simpler demands on all
concerned: a promoter would find a field, build a stage and invite some
bands to perform. A few ads in the underground press, a buzz on the word-
of-mouth network and the people would come. Some paid the pound or
so admission charge, while others saw music as their birthright and broke
down the fences, letting thousands more enter.

The global phenomenon that was Woodstock, and the resultant Oscar-winning movie, inspired small town and city youth from all classes and backgrounds, to seek a re-creation of the Woodstock spirit closer to home. Held the summer after Woodstock, the 1970 Isle of Wight festival was even bigger in scale than its American cousin, and said to be one of the biggest human gatherings ever held. With a line-up including The Doors, The Who and Jimi Hendrix, tens of thousands arrived without tickets, and, encouraged by an anarchic element set on keeping music free for the people, they broke down the flimsy fences and turned the event into a reluctant free festival.

The ensuing public order concerns were debated in Parliament and culminated with an act being passed in 1971 requiring future festivals on the island to seek a special licence – but it was too late: the festival was abandoned.

THE SEVENTIES

It was also in the summer of 1970 that Somerset farmer Michael Eavis, influenced by the Isle of Wight festival, decided to stage a little event of his own. The Pilton Festival, as it was called, was headlined by T. Rex and attended by 1,500 people. Initially reluctant

to repeat the exercise, Eavis was persuaded to make it an annual event by the festivalgoers who loved it so much they didn't want it to end. Glastonbury Fayre was born.

But, during the 1970s, it was all about Reading. Knebworth had the Stones and Pink Floyd, but was essentially a one-day gig with a forced overnight stop for most fans. On the other hand, Reading lasted the whole August bank holiday weekend, with Monday to recover. The Reading Festival was finely tuned into the rock zeitgeist by then, and thousands travelled to the riverside site to eat hot dogs, drink beer and watch bands like The Faces, Thin Lizzy and Aerosmith.

But the hippies bemoaned the creeping commercialization of events like Reading, and a parallel free festival movement blossomed at the same time. Hippies, anarchists, bikers and Hare Krishnas would get together mainly by word-of-mouth to enjoy nakedness, substances, bonfires and music. Facilities were generally non-existent, or perhaps someone would stay straight long enough to dig a toilet, and what food there was, was shared.

Some free festivals, such as Bury's Deeply Vale, passed off peacefully, while others, notably Windsor in 1974, were violently broken up by police.

The biggest free festival was, of course, at Stonehenge, which ran for 14 years and served up a 'happening', with all bands and all free-minded individuals invited to turn up and join in. Hawkwind, Here and Now and Roy Harper played and there was a collection for the free food.

> **Top tip for first-time festivalgoers**
> *My top festival tip for festival virgins is to ditch your mates for a bit and have a wander. I did this when I was 16 and went and did loads of funky dancing to Cornershop. It was very liberating!*
> **Sally, Leeds**

> **What was your first festival experience?**
> *Stonehenge Free Festival in 1977 which was great because it was all free. The music was free too although the only band I remember playing there was Hawkwind. It had a great atmosphere, no trouble and a low police presence despite the abundance of drugs.*
> **Andrew, Southampton**

EARLY EIGHTIES

The 1984 festival brought 30,000 punks and alternative folks to the stones, and it appeared to be a victim of its own success. The authorities banned the next year's event. The subsequent Battle of the

MAKE POVERTY HIST

Top tip for first-time festivalgoers
Always take wellies, lots of soap-free baby wipes and dry bin liners or carrier bags for your clothes. And your own portable camping loo if you can.
Jon, Winchester

Beanfield, which saw a convoy of live-in vehicles trashed by riot police and new-age travellers injured in an early-morning raid, has gone down in counter-culture history as a turning point for the festival movement under Thatcherism.

THE EIGHTIES AND NINETIES

For the free festival movement, much of the rest of the eighties and early nineties seemed to be spent being shifted around by police enforcing the new Public Order Acts, which banned gatherings on public land. Meanwhile, the Elephant Fayre in Cornwall, which had grown steadily from small roots to become a regular and much-loved commercial festival, was abandoned in 1986 after some travellers – far removed from the peaceful hippies of the early movement – tried to storm the fence to get in free.

By the eighties, the eclectic bills of the early Reading Festivals had been replaced by wall-to-wall hard rock and metal. Then in 1988, the Mean Fiddler organization staged a coup and secured the licence to run a festival on the Reading site. This was followed by the demise of the Mean Fiddler's own Phoenix Festival, which ran from 1993 to 1997, but was marred by overbearing security, campsite violence and high prices. When the 1998 Phoenix was cancelled, some of the acts moved to the Reading bill.

Under new promoters, the Reading Festival set the standard for festivals in the nineties and beyond. Bands plucked from the pages of the music press were booked, and multiple stages, a festival market, food outlets and a funfair were introduced – while admission prices steadily increased.

The Glastonbury Festival was now the main hippyish alternative to the grunge of Reading. Michael Eavis allowed displaced travellers to hold their own festival adjacent to the site after Stonehenge was banned – until again trouble from the convoy in 1990 led to a mini-riot and a future ban.

In the nineties, four distinct subgroups of festivals emerged. The hippy-style free festivals continued, but against constant police and government pressure. As a result, many were shut down or moved on by roadblocks.

Meanwhile the rave movement held their own style free events at secret locations often accessible from the M25, using mobile phones to pass out last-minute venue details. Castlemorton Free Festival in 1992 was a combination of both: a sleepy village in the Malvern Hills was shocked by the influx of 40,000 old-style hippies and ecstasy-fuelled ravers with sound systems, live stages and their associated detritus.

Middle England agreed: free festivals were a threat to society. The Criminal Justice Act of 1993 effectively outlawed such gatherings, giving the police powers to seize equipment and arrest organizers.

The clampdown served to boost legal festivals. Glastonbury grew and grew. Always a haven for alternatives, it increasingly became a focus for people with leftfield views, beliefs and lifestyles; a legal outlet for the festival urge. The event mutated into a linked system of festival villages, all on one sprawling site, but each with its own individual lifestyle and *raison d'être*.

> **What was your most surreal festival moment?**
> *Three guys crawling through the crowd on hands and knees gibbering about how the Mooks were coming and Mooks were bad. This was during the Bjork set on the NME stage, so may have been related to that rather than drugs.*
> **Lance, Norwich**

TODAY

More mainstream commercial festivals went from strength to strength. Reading was joined by Phoenix, V Festival and T in the Park as annual events, and the south of England no longer held the monopoly on big-scale festivals. When Glastonbury organizers gave the festival a miss in 1991 and 1996, they left the field clear for alternatives. But it wasn't just the big events that benefited – smaller events with niche audiences started to spring up to cater for those who sought a more intimate festival experience. They flocked to the niche events that targeted a particular audience, like the psychedelic revival of the Canterbury Fayre or the family-friendly and bijou Larmer Tree in Wiltshire.

Today, unless you plan months ahead, you will be hard pushed to get a ticket for a major festival. The underground days are far behind and the Reading, Leeds and Glasto are as much part of England's summer social whirl as Wimbledon and the FA Cup Final.

The major television networks now beam live from all the top events to your living room or computer screen – or maybe internet fans would prefer to take part in a virtual festival on Second Life.

Despite the stay-at-home alternatives and despite the dodgy weather, more than a million of us will attend a festival in the UK in 2008. Times may change, the tents and the music may change, but the pull of tents and mud and rock and roll remains the same.

That festive feeling

'There is something about a festival which no other musical event offers, the smoke of the campfires, the marathon element of coming back again and again to the stages day after day, the sense of freedom one has in a large campsite or arena and the buzz one gets off the music in the outdoor setting that does not seem to exist in the confines of the conventional concert hall or club.'
The Great White Shark, www.ukrockfestivals.com

Festivals are a bit like Marmite: you either love them or hate them; few people stand somewhere in-between. Those who get the festival bug keep coming back, the advancement of years and the addition of small children merely signalling a shift in the type of event attended or the particular stage most frequented. Even those who fall off the festival radar for a few years tend to creep back, to one-day events or a tentative Guilfest, new family and new tent in tow, checking reactions to see if this could make a feasible alternative to a weekend at the seaside.

But for Brits who can't get enough of festivals, what makes us love them so much? Despite our unpredictable summers, festivals have never been so popular. Ask anyone who has been to a washed-out event what it was like, the probable answer will be 'despite the weather, it was fantastic'.

Some people stick to one favourite annual event each year, really letting rip in glow sticks, costumes and daft dancing for three days, the rest of the year living unremarkable lives. Others, like the Croissant Neuf crew, have found a niche in festival provision that enables them to dedicate themselves full-time to being part of the festival vibe. Another type of festival fan will forego a fortnight in the sun in favour of buying tickets for every major festival event from Glastonbury to Reading.

What all these people have in common is a love of the atmosphere found only at festivals and a need to be a part of it, to the extent that jammed booking lines, long traffic queues or summer storms conspire but fail to dampen their spirit. Festivals are a British institution, but once part of one, it's another Britain you're in: a friendlier, less reserved and more hedonistic one, an alternative universe where making a living is not important, but having fun is paramount.

FREEDOM

The most important part of the festival vibe is the freedom – to forget about the hassles that get us down in everyday life,

---

What was your most surreal festival experience?

1990 at Glastonbury I saw a Rastafarian guy, probably around 50 years old, dreadlocks and beard greying, with a piece of string tied round his wrist connecting him to his wife, who was in turn connected to the tallest child, then second child, third child and finally came the dog. A strange enough sight on its own – made even stranger by them all being stark naked.
Tony, Hartlepool

like our jobs, college, sometimes even families. Festival freedom allows us to dress and dance as we like, be as mature or immature as we please, enjoy a drink or a smoke without having to drive home afterwards – and to meet like-minded people from all over with the same intentions and values.

In our alternative festival universe, people like to seize the opportunity to reinvent themselves, with a festival personality and sometimes even a new festival name. Travel with a group of people you think you know well and observe these strange transformations at first hand: the mainstream rock fan getting stoned and spending hours digging acid jazz; the meek office worker stripping down to body paint for the whole weekend, and the two old friends getting it together for the first time because they've finally left their inhibitions behind.

ADVENTURE

Festivalgoing is an expedition, a trip, an adventure into the unknown. Every festival is different, and yet they have elements in common that are seductive, even addictive. The sense of adventure – to watch bands and performances you've never encountered before, to put yourself at the mercy of an alternative healer in Glastonbury's Green Fields, or even to try a takeaway from a country you've never heard of – is a feeling that is hard to replicate while still staying within the UK, even if in reality you're only straying slightly from your personal comfort zone.

SIMPLICITY

The simplicity of festivals, especially the smaller events, is liberating too. Forget the TV, work and the constant thud of bills popping through your letterbox. Small tasks, like getting clean water to cook with, take us back to a forgotten age, when not everything was on tap. A hay bale is a much-appreciated seat in a world largely without furniture, and a hot cup of tea from a stall first thing in the morning is little short of a miracle.

When you are eating, drinking and playing outdoors most of the time, you're bound to feel closer to nature. No matter how good your camping set-up, you will be spending most of your time out in the elements.

Couples get together at festivals – just about as often as couples split up. The forced intimacy of sharing a piece of canvas for 72 hours can make or break relationships. If the lack of hair straighteners or Sky Sports is more important than being together, the chances are this will become apparent at some point during the weekend.

Families can enjoy each other's company, free from the various pulls of different interests and timetables. A kids' area adjoining the main stage (Beautiful Days sometimes has this) is a case in point. Junior sploshes away with paint and crayons while parent sits nearby, one eye on the unfolding masterpiece and another on the ska band ripping it up on the stage.

Life-long memories can be made and shared between groups of friends at festivals. Student gangs can stage reunions at the same festival for years after graduation, the event possibly providing the link back to rose-tinted, more carefree times.

Looking to be part of a bigger picture, a tribe or a movement is a natural instinct in today's urbanized society, and a festival – especially if it's a special interest one or if it's offering a particular type of music – can provide that feeling of belonging and community, even if it's just for a couple of days.

On the web, festival message boards keep each festival's fan community going throughout the year, with postings on all topics under the sun – not least speculation on who's going to be headlining the following year. Message board meet-ups happen at all festivals, and individuals who have chatted and argued online all year finally meet up over a beer.

THE FUTURE

But what of the future? Festivals are diverging in three distinct areas:

• The major commercial events, professionally organized and catered and featuring top bands. If these events judge the market right, they sell out in hours. People get to see large numbers of top bands in a very short space of time, but concerns are high prices, overbearing security and petty crime.

• Smaller boutique festivals, including one-day events and themed parties, sometimes slickly organized, but often eschewing commercial sponsorship in favour of a more rootsy approach, with standards to match. When all goes well they can be fantastic parties, but in a crisis, such as terrible weather or power failure, everything can go pear-shaped pretty quickly.

• Green events, where festivals focus on the fringe side of festival life: the camps, the cafés, alternative communities, sustainable living, spirituality and cooperation. The most commercial of these is the Big Green Gathering, but, taken to extremes, a true rainbow gathering will have no admission fee, no organizers and no money will be exchanged throughout the event. At this point the central element of most festivals – the music – no longer matters and what entertainment there is tends to be amateur and spontaneous.

As the festival scene diversifies, splits and continues to grow, mass acceptance of this type of entertainment is higher than ever. Who among the 3,000 people who attended the first Glastonbury Festival would have thought that in 2008 a festival nearly a hundred times its size would be taking place in the same fields, and simultaneously broadcast to millions on the BBC? Would they even have liked that idea?

Nowadays, there is nothing radical about attending and enjoying a festival, although part of the fun is pretending that there is. The fact is, you're as likely to rub shoulders with fellow music fans who happen to be off-duty police officers as you are to encounter the undercover drug squad. Free Hare Krishna food competes as a marketing tool with free samples of Linda McCartney ready meals, and the queues for the ATMs are at least as long as the latrine queues. But it's still better than staying at home ...

Making a difference

Francis Rossi, Status Quo, on performing at Live Aid: 'With a large audience like that you do usually get a good vibe, but there was something totally unique and I'm not sure I've ever felt it since. They weren't just people paying to see a show, they were part of it. There was such a euphoric feeling in that arena.'

Not festivals as such, major 'cause' concerts walk the line between music gig and political rally, buoyed along on a wave of collective goodwill whipped up by common purpose.

The first large-scale benefit was George Harrison's Concert for Bangladesh, a post-hippy superstar blow-out at New York's Madison Square Gardens in 1971. The concert and subsequent album and movies raised more than £7.5 million, but the US government held most of the profit in a tax account, rather than it going to the people of Bangladesh.

In the mid-eighties, Live Aid, a one-day, 16-hour spectacular at London's Wembley Stadium and JFK Stadium in Philadelphia, with other simultaneous concerts worldwide, was televised to 1.5 billion viewers and raised

The Black Eyed Peas on stage for Live Earth in 2007

$100 million for charity. Joan Baez introduced the Philadelphia show as the new Woodstock – and it was long overdue.

A succession of follow-ups was held at the Wembley Stadium, including the Nelson Mandela 70th Birthday Tribute (1988), and the Freddie Mercury AIDS Benefit in 1992. Wembley concerts

attract a much more mainstream crowd than a typical festival might, and there is little room in such monster line-ups for up-and-coming acts.

In the 21st century, the focus moved from fundraising to awareness-raising, with the Live 8 series of concerts for the Make Poverty History campaign and 2007's Live Earth concerts against global warming. The relative flop of Live Earth, both in television viewing figures and the backlash against the environmental cost of putting on the concerts, could mean there will be a trend towards more low-key events, with political causes adopting a grass-roots approach to getting their message across to people. Festivals would seem the natural home for such initiatives – watch this space!

Major Festivals

Glastonbury
the daddy of them all

It would be unthinkable to talk about festivals
these days without mentioning Glastonbury.
After all, it's the biggest, most diverse and by far
the most oversubscribed event on the festival calendar.
And it's been going since 1970.

For several years now hundreds of thousands of people have sat by the phone, fingers of one hand on redial, the other hand pressing refresh on the online booking page on their computer. And many fail to get tickets. Yet they'll be doing the same again next year, because they've got to get through sometime. No one back in 1986 would believe how Glastonbury has grown, both in size and demand (see page 9).

For many years, festivalgoers either booked when they had money, paid on the gate, or simply jumped the fence. The event was at best tolerated by the local Somerset community, and at worst actively opposed. Founder and organizer Michael Eavis, a dairy farmer, hosted the first event without any plans for a repeat, but he was persuaded to change his mind by the hippies who had enjoyed the festival and demanded more of the same. Eavis, who oozes down-to-earth charm, worked relentlessly on the locals for years, offering them work and free tickets, and doing his best to convince the conservative authorities that Glastonbury Fayre (as it was then known) should continue.

Back in the seventies and early eighties, there was Reading for the rock crowd, Stonehenge for the alternative types, and Glastonbury was seen by some as a middle ground – a bit chin-stroking and a little bit, well, wet – not exactly cutting-edge. When the Stonehenge Free Festival was banned in 1985 and the travellers' attempts at partying were violently opposed by the police (see the Battle of the Beanfield, pages 7–8), it was at Glastonbury that the battered veterans sought sanctuary. Eavis accommodated the displaced

Michael Eavis and some typical Glastonbury weather

travellers, and for the next few years Glasto grew and developed an atmosphere somewhere between a Moroccan souk, a medieval fair, *Mad Max* and the cantina from the first Star Wars movie, with the music almost incidental.

As Glasto has grown, the quality of its musical line-up has improved, with world-class acts such as The Who and Paul McCartney vying for headline slots on the main Pyramid Stage, hot new bands playing career-making sets on the NME stage, and gonzo performances taking place unannounced all over the site by household names in music, theatre and comedy for the lucky few who manage to find them by accident or word-of-mouth. Ironically, the growing expectation of great entertainment has contributed to the festival selling out almost instantly in recent years – months before any acts are confirmed.

Weatherwise, Glastonbury has been quite literally on sticky ground; its late June slot is the first major weekend of the festival season, and before summer kicks in properly. Its hilly site is vulnerable to flooding, bogs and tent-piercing icy winds at night. But in a good year, when the sun shines

What was your best ever festival and why?
Probably Glastonbury 1983. The weather was great as was the line up. I was a big Van Morrison fan at the time who did a fantastic set right after The Chieftains. Probably the reason I remember it so fondly was the fact I ended up sharing a tent with a friend's girlfriend. At the end of three days she was my girlfriend!
Andrew, Southampton

The entire Glastonbury site is a hive of activity for the festival

and the rain stays away, you simply cannot beat it. There is so much going on beyond the music that you can find a good spot to sit just about anywhere on site, and let the festival come to you – from stilt-walkers dressed as policemen, elderly transvestites chatting into bananas held to their ear, random parades, and the irrepressible tide of borderline entrepreneurs, selling everything from vodka jelly shots to Welsh magic mushrooms and tarot readings.

The festival's capacity currently stands at 177,500 ticket holders. That of course doesn't count all the under-12s who get in for free, the massive festival crew, thousands of performers, media, and the traders who book well ahead for the privilege of catering to the festival crowd. In other words, for a week in June, the tiny village of Pilton hosts a tent city bigger than Newcastle. And that's a city where most of the inhabitants are at least squiffy, possibly legless and potentially very, very stoned.

What is it that makes Glasto so special? Partly it's the festival's origins as a homespun charity event seemingly at odds with commercial rock and roll, and its very visible support for good causes like CND, and more recently Greenpeace, Oxfam and Water Aid. The strong bias towards green issues, with recycling, renewable-energy sources and just about any environmental pressure group represented in the Green Fields adds to the worthiness of the event. And finally the location is superb – just a few miles down the road from the mystical Glastonbury Tor, in an area heavy with myth and legend, ley lines and tales of dragons, knights and the Holy Grail.

Even a thorough guide to Glastonbury can't list every stage. It's that big. In 2008, expect about 50 venues where you can see music played, either live or by DJs, plus all the cabaret, circus, comedy and other non-musical entertainments on offer.

GLASTONBURY SITE MAP

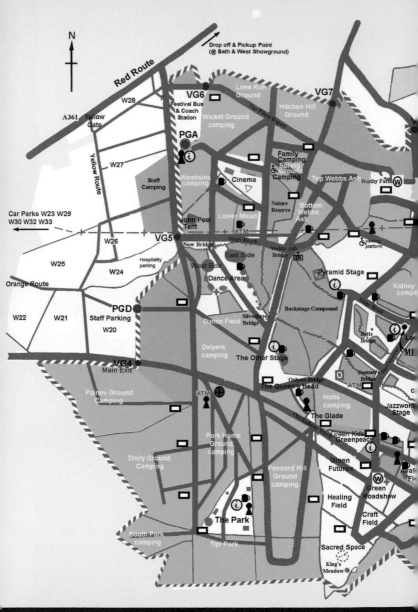

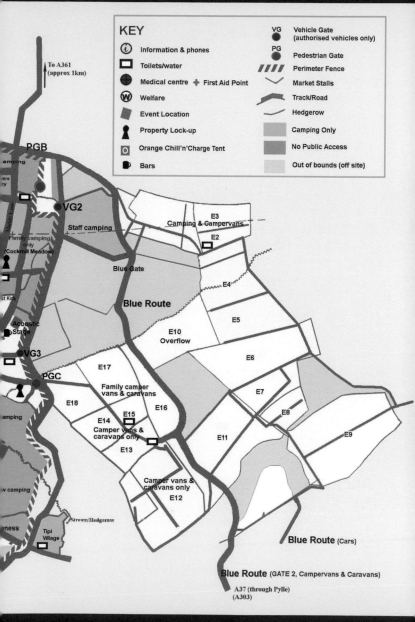

KEY

ⓘ Information & phones

▢ Toilets/water

◉ Medical centre ✚ First Aid Point

Ⓦ Welfare

▮ Event Location

♟ Property Lock-up

Ⓞ Orange Chill'n'Charge Tent

🍺 Bars

VG ● Vehicle Gate (authorised vehicles only)

PG ● Pedestrian Gate

//// Perimeter Fence

∨ Market Stalls

▬ Track/Road

〜 Hedgerow

▨ Camping Only

▨ No Public Access

▨ Out of bounds (off site)

To A361 (approx 1km)

PGB
amping
ntre
y
●VG2
Staff camping
Family camping only (Cockmill Meadow)
Blue Gate
st Kids
Acoustic Stage s
●VG3
PGC
E17
Family camper vans & caravans
E18
E14
Camper vans & caravans only
E15
E16
E13
amping
w camping
eness
Tipi Village
Stream/Hedgerow

E3
Camping & Campervans
E2
E4
Blue Route
E10 Overflow
E5
E6
E7
E8
E11
E9
Camper vans & caravans only
E12

Blue Route (Cars)

Blue Route (GATE 2, Campervans & Caravans)

A37 (through Pylle)
(A303)

23

If you are an early bird arriving on the Wednesday before the event officially kicks off, you will still find stuff going on – but you will be hard-pressed to see everything, even if you stay for the full five days.

As in any city, Glastonbury is a series of connected neighourhoods, each with its own population and character. Although officially Britain's biggest festival, the problem of Glastonbury's size means that you have to take it in bite-sized chunks – a morning in the Green Futures field, for example, before chilling out at the Jazzworld Stage in the afternoon and heading to Lost Vagueness for a night of dancing. Others pick an area and stay for the duration.

> **What was your first festival experience? Was it what you expected?**
> *Glastonbury 1994. It was not what I expected. In fact it was a million times better and everything changed once I returned home. There was so much there and so many friendly people. It turned into a completely different scene once the sun went down.*
> **Dave, Chichester**

Regulars try to camp in the same spot each year and meet up with like-minded individuals. The hills near the Pyramid Stage have a reputation for large groups of drunken lads, with commercial tastes in music and a disinclination for sleep whatever the hour. The Green Fields have a gentler feel, with a more alternative crowd and a greater tolerance for eccentric behaviour. The family and camper van fields attract an older, more festival-weary crowd, who want to enjoy themselves but not at the expense of a good night's sleep and like to bring home comforts along.

If your only experience of Glasto has been watching the BBC's extensive coverage of the acts on the Pyramid Stage, prepare to be shocked at the diversity of entertainment, and the scale of the event way beyond the big headline stages.

AROUND THE FESTIVAL

PYRAMID STAGE. The festival's landmark, the Pyramid Stage is of course the biggest stage with the largest crowd and the most famous performers. It's set at the bottom of a shallow valley, and the Pyramid crowd swells throughout the day until the whole area is jammed for the evening's headliners. Getting to and from this stage is an absolute nightmare from early evening onwards – best stay put or give it a miss. This is the stage you are most likely to see on television.

THE OTHER STAGE. If you're hanging out with a group of friends, prepare to have a major argument about which stage to be at each evening. The Other Stage boasts bands that would easily headline the main stage at any other festival. Headliners in 2007 included Björk, Iggy and the Stooges and the Chemical Brothers. Back to back with the Pyramid Stage, you can just about dash between the two if you're nimble.

JOHN PEEL STAGE. Everyone's favourite festival DJ and MC, John Peel used to hang out at the New Tent between presenting slots on the BBC festival coverage. When he sadly died in 2004, Michael Eavis renamed the tent in his honour. Here you'll find a mixture of new and breakthrough acts with the odd legend making an appearance. This is where you are most likely to catch next year's big thing.

JAZZWORLD STAGE. Brilliant in sunshine, with its colourful flags, uplifting sounds and mellow vibe, Jazzworld fills the aural void between the guitar-based main stages and the Dance Village. This is the domain of classy singers such as Corinne Bailey Rae, Amy Winehouse and Joss Stone; and virtuoso musicians, solo, backed by big bands or even full orchestras.

AND THEN OF COURSE THERE ARE ...
ACOUSTIC TENT. On its own hillside, this tented stage aims for a timeless feel. We are talking amplified acoustic and famous names rather than a buskers' haven. Acts who have performed recently include the Waterboys,

Richard Thompson and Alison Moyet. Close to the Kidz Field, it's popular with families but gets uncomfortably busy when favourite acts are onstage, so many people choose to picnic outside.

DANCE VILLAGE. An area dedicated to beats and boogie. Two main tents – East and West – each able to handle around 2,000 ravers, a hip hop tent, plus a plush lounge, and an outdoor DJ stage. When everything else shuts down, grab your glow sticks, slap on your headphones and get down in the Silent Disco.

Is this tent much bigger on the inside?

THE GLADE. So successful that the organizers now run their own festival, this dance/electronic/ambient area is in, and makes a feature of, the woods. With its own bar and café, there's a chilled-out atmosphere and loyal followers.

THEATRE AND CIRCUS FIELDS. When the music gets all too much, you can seek all manner of alternative entertainment in these three fields, from traditional circus to the futuristic biker landscape of Trash City, hosted by the Mutoid Waste Co. and featuring their trademark kinetic metal structures. If you feel the need for high culture, dance companies perform among the clowns and there are daily doses of Shakespeare.

THE LEFT FIELD. Not a field at all but a huge tent and satellite structures under a large metal tower near the main meeting point, the Left Field describes itself as the social conscience of Glastonbury. Organized by Battersea and Wandsworth Trades Council, expect a mixture of political

Jo Whiley co-hosted BBC TV's 2007 coverage

debate, comedy, Battle of the Bands winners and some surprisingly big names such as Babyshambles, Lethal Bizzle and Joss Stone, plus legends like Steve Earle and Jerry Dammers onstage with their bands. It's not all beer and sandwiches though – the Left Field Bar does a mean cocktail.

DON'T FORGET TO JOURNEY TO THE OUTER REACHES ...

GREEN FIELDS. Occupying a third of the entire festival site, the Green Fields are where many feel the true Glastonbury spirit resides. Think alternative sources of energy – the wind, the sun and bicycles are employed here to power the sound systems. The food is GM-free and generally vegetarian, the tepee village provides living theatre, and the Healing Field is where to go for relief of aches, pains and spiritual malaise. You'll also find bands performing on the many Green stages; and of course at King's Meadow, overlooking the festival site is the Stone Circle, built in 1990 but looking for all the world as if it has been there for aeons, where crowds welcome the sunrise each morning and where the burnt-out look down on the rest of the festival and recharge their batteries.

LOST VAGUENESS. As the Green Fields are natural and mellow, so Lost Vagueness is brash and chaotic. This field, which is dedicated to all things kitsch, glam and decadent, turns the whole festival experience on its head by offering luxury Airstream trailer accommodation at far from trailer-park prices, operating a dress code in its ballroom and casino (as well as a changing room where you can swap your festival duds for hired dinner suits and burlesque finery), and offering a Vegas-style wedding chapel where loved-up festival fans can tie the knot. Probably to the later relief of some over-enthusiastic couples, the vows are not legally binding. After hours, the chapel becomes a cabaret with DJs and novelty acts.

THE PARK. Emily Eavis's baby, The Park is the Glastonbury heiress's stab at putting her own mark on her dad's festival. Only started in 2007, The Park is a long slog from the main areas but worth the trek, as it combines all the highlights of the whole festival in one space – and has pianos!

All this and there are still the bars, the amazing range of food and market stalls, the Gay Disco, the Fire Corner, the huge outdoor cinema, the amazing Kidz Field, and the Late 'N' Live tent. Not to mention the 20 or so smaller stages that you have to stumble across to know about, or the fantastic dub reggae coming from that coffee stall you spent hours at on the first day but haven't been able to find since.

> **What was your most surreal festival moment?**
> *Being growled at by a duffel coat-wearing Thom Yorke in front of the NME stage at Glastonbury '94. I'd been staring at his huge bottle of cider – and he was wearing a duffel coat in the middle of a sun-baked afternoon. Half an hour later he took to the stage and I discovered who Radiohead were. I promptly forgot them again and found Back To The Planet in the travellers' field instead.*
> **Dave, Chichester**

If anything, Glastonbury has too much going on. No two experiences of this festival will be alike and no one, no matter how well organized, will get round everything. But that's not what Glastonbury is about after all. In the words of Michael Eavis himself:

'Hurrying between stages so you can tick off a list of things you feel you must see is not the best way to enjoy Glastonbury. If you can't get a good vantage point, or aren't enjoying a show, move on. There'll be something else in the next field! You might not have heard of it before, but often your best memories will be of new things that startle you with their brilliance, rather than checking whether idols live up to expectations.'

MORE INFORMATION

The official Glastonbury site (www.glastonburyfestivals.co.uk) is almost as sprawling and interesting as the event itself. The message boards are a great place to hook up with new friends, ask newbie questions and keep the Glasto spirit alive 365 days of the year.

You'll also find plenty of information, chiefly about the main stages and camping conditions, at http://news.bbc.co.uk and www.nme.com.

Download

If you've got hair, denim and a penchant for ear-bleeding metal music, you'll already know what Download is.

The offspring of the legendary Donington Monsters of Rock one-day hard rock festivals of the eighties and nineties, young upstart Download, first held in 2003, is now a fully fledged, on-site camping metal-fest with a 70,000 capacity, and is a must for rock fans.

Featuring three stages and a range of acts that run the gamut from metal to, umm, hard rock, Download knows its audience, and its audience knows what to expect from the festival. Each year, there is much speculation in the rock press as to which bands will meet with disapproval from the Download crowd. Indie rockers Feeder won them over in 2005, but the next year, Axl Rose and his reconstituted Guns 'n' Roses were bottled almost to the point of abandoning their set.

Megadeth kicked off the 2007 festival

Within Download's self-imposed musical margins, the festival often serves up treats and surprises, both planned and unplanned. In 2004, Metallica's drummer Lars Urlich was taken ill en route to the festival, and, rather than pull their headline slot, the rest of the band played what is acclaimed as one of their best gigs ever. They rounded up on-site drummers from Slayer and Slipknot to fill in. Two years later, Korn's vocalist Jonathan Davies was rushed to hospital before the band was due to take to the main stage. In proper Download spirit, the band played anyway, with the help of half a dozen impromptu guest vocalists from other bands on the bill.

Download has established itself over the past five years as a metal fan's essential festival, and the line-up has consistently reflected the best in metal, hard rock and thrash, with occasional forays into the world of emo (My Chemical Romance headlined one night in 2007) and goth rock. The more adventurous sounds are to be heard in one of the smaller arenas, the latest of which is the Dimebag Darrell stage, named after the former Pantera singer who was gunned down onstage in 2005 (though thankfully not at Download) by a disgruntled fan.

With three main stages (watch out for the mosh pits!), a new bands area, cinema and fairground, as well as campsite parties after hours and the occasional five-a-side football match in the afternoons, Download has grown up to be a proper festival weekend.

LINKS
Donington Park, Derbyshire
13–15 June
www.downloadfestival.co.uk

Isle of Wight

Organizer John Giddings seems to have a golden touch when it comes to booking bands, making the Isle of Wight a cut above in the line-up stakes.

Trading on a rich history of legendary performances in the hippy era (The Who, Jimi Hendrix, Miles Davis, The Doors, to mention a few), today's Isle of Wight Festival is not the sort of place where a free-loving, gatecrashing longhair could just wander in.

The iconic, if shambolic, events of the original Isle of Wight festivals were consigned to the annals of rock history until 2002, when a new festival (that year named Rock Island) drew 8,000 people back to the island. Since then, the Isle of Wight Festival, which apart from its name shares only a romantic association with its hippy predecessor, has been steadily growing, with 70,000 watching The Rolling Stones headline in 2007.

Organizers play on the psychedelic heritage of the festival (they bought a Hendrix statue for the Isle of Wight last year), but are happy to have the event sponsored by business corporations.

As with Bestival, the other island festival, the cost of the ferry bumps up the price quite a bit (although Isle of Wight ferry companies offer early bird discount tickets). This is another festival that always sells out in advance.

As well as The Stones, Giddings has managed to convince Coldplay to headline soon after they announced that they were taking a break, he's reunited The Police, tempted David Bowie across the Solent and brought The Who back here.

LINKS
13–15 June
www.isleofwightfestival.com

Oxegen

Ireland's biggest festival was previously called Witnness, and has run since 2000.

Since being renamed in 2004, Oxegen has been held at Punchestown Racecourse, Naas, in Kildare. More than 80,000 fans a day come to the festival, with half of these day tickets, the other half camping onsite.

Snow Patrol entertaining the Oxegen crowd

Oxegen is informally twinned with Scotland's T in The Park, sharing many of the acts over the same weekend.

Only 40 kilometres (25 miles) from Dublin, and easily accessible by shuttle buses, Oxegen entices in thousands of music fans from the UK and mainland Europe, who want to see the big-name bands on the festival circuit but have been unlucky getting Glastonbury or Reading tickets – although Oxegen is becoming a fast seller too: 2007's tickets sold out before any acts were announced.

Oxegen facts
Helping festivalgoers were:
200 gardai (police) at two garda stations
2,000 security personnel
250 medics

Over two days and six stages, the level of quality music is consistently high, with acts from both sides of the Irish Sea well represented, as well as edgy US acts (2007 saw The Killers, Queens of the Stone Age, Scissor Sisters and My Chemical Romance appearing).

All the usual extras are laid on, from the funfair to the comedy tent and the dance arena, and there are even supermarkets in the colour-coded campsites. There are also free hot showers and a separate site for family camping, although the festival organizers don't encourage or lay on facilities for under-fives (under-17s have to be accompanied by an adult who will sign up to looking after and being responsible for them at all times).

LINKS

Naas, Kildare, Ireland
11–13 July
www.oxegen.ie

Reading and Leeds

They say you know you're getting old when policemen
start looking young, but that's nothing on the
reality-check anyone over 25 gets at Reading
and Leeds these days.

These twin festivals, held simultaneously with virtually the same line-up
over the August bank holiday weekend, are a magnet for sixth formers,
students and their younger siblings celebrating their GCSE results with a
weekend of NME-friendly rock and roll. Anyone younger is going to get
bored: although kids get in free, there's nothing here for them. Anyone
older is going to feel ancient, all weekend.

EARLY DAYS

It was not always thus. Squeezing out a bit of facial hair may be beyond
most of the enthusiastic crowd of fresh-faced, Foo Fighters T'd teenagers,
but some of their predecessors at Readings gone by were hirsute enough
to attract the attention of Sir David Attenborough.

Today's first-time festivalgoers at Reading may not realize it, but they
are part of a long tradition that goes right back to the dawn of time in UK
festival history. Their grandparents may well have been among the hip
crowd who flocked to the original National
Jazz and Blues festivals in the sixties, to
give it up for The Stones and The
Yardbirds, and their parents may well have
been part of the boozed-up crowd who
head-banged to Iron Maiden on the same
Caversham site back in 1980 ...

EVOLUTION

By the time the festival had found its
permanent home in Reading 1970, blues
and jazz had been eclipsed by hippy-
friendly rock music, and the stage was set

for the seventies. The Reading Festival, as it became known, was a fixture in the summer festival calendar throughout the seventies and early eighties, seeing off short-lived events along the way.

After a brief flirtation with 'New Wave' acts in the late seventies, with the inevitable clashes between punks and metallers onsite, the organizers played it safe and for a few years in the early eighties the festival became a metal and hard rock event. In many ways Reading was a parody of itself – the homebrew got stronger, the denim got more faded and the Salvation Army tent was hard-pressed to hand out blankets each night for the armies of fans who had turned up with plenty of beer but no tent. Among the popular-music press, the word was that Reading was irrelevant to the music of the day. Not that Reading regulars noticed.

Back then, anyone who dared stand close to the stage ran a high risk of being hit on the back of the head with a bottle full of pee. These unsavoury missiles came in two versions: lid off and lid on. The first created a shower that, while pleasantly cooling at first, once identified, drew screams of disgust from an already belligerent crowd. The second type, a heavy, targeted missile, would take out individual members of the audience, who would fall down and rise again, barely registering concussion on top of their ongoing drunken, semi-coherent state.

Welcome to Reading, old-style, where B-list rock acts such as Saxon entertained hairy, denim-clad crowds, with little reference to the popular music trends of the day. It was a 'lads' festival', where long queues wound in front of hot dog and cider vans, while adjacent tofu stir-fry offerings

went untested; where a popular game was spotting undercover Thames Valley drugs squad officers, hysterically dressed in pressed jeans, rugby shirts and shiny Doc Martens, their neat hair and trimmed moustaches a dead giveaway

The winner was the first punter to stand in front of the identified undercover, bend comically at the knee and say 'Ev'nin' all' to his face, while grinning with a lit joint in his mouth, then running away into the crowd. Oh how we laughed!

READING TODAY

Hey, that was a long time past. Twenty years ago, the festival was wrested from its long-time organizers in a coup by the Mean Fiddler organization (now Festival Republic) and reborn. It's easy to see why. Despite the festival's dodgy reputation both on and off stage, the location – flat parkland a short walk from town and a station that connects to London Paddington in half an hour – was the real prize.

> **What was your most surreal festival moment?**
> I have seen many strange characters and had many strange experiences.
> At Reading 2006, whilst working on a disabled viewing platform I had a request: 'I don't want to use the platform, but can I stand behind the barrier, I was circumcised a couple of days ago and I'm still sore'. This was one of those times I took the customer's word rather than ask him to prove it.
> **Tony, Hartlepool**

Under the new promoter, a revamped Reading Festival took shape, which forms the basis of the festival you see today. Out went dinosaur rock bands and in came Dinosaur Jr – booking inspiration now coming from the pages of *NME* rather than *Kerrang!* magazine.

Reading brought grunge, Britpop and Indie to a wide audience, with notable appearances from Nirvana (who played their final UK gig at Reading), The Stone Roses, The Prodigy, Suede and Blur in the nineties.

The limited semi-urban site of the Reading Festival has meant that while its popularity has increased, its capacity hasn't – so tickets have been selling out faster and faster. In 2007, the tickets sold out within two hours. In response the organizers started a northern twin: Carling Weekend Leeds, which shares the same line-up but on different nights over the weekend.

Today at Reading, if you manage to get hold of tickets, you can expect a feast of credible yet million-selling bands and comeback artists,

supported by most of the music press's latest cool list. In 2007, headline slots went to The Red Hot Chilli Peppers and Smashing Pumpkins plus the UK's Razorlight.

The second stage is currently sponsored by Radio One and features some of the top newer bands on the rock and Indie scene. Further stages include the Carling Stage (breakthrough acts) and the Radio One Lock Up Stage, for more underground music. Dance music features on one night at each festival and a comedy tent draws names from TV and the club circuit.

CAMPING

This festival is generally strictly organized, with separate arena and campsite areas. The location means that music in the arena has to finish at set times. In 2007 all-night entertainment was introduced in the purple campsite, alongside a bar, market, a silent disco and cafés.

You can buy tickets by the day, or stay for the weekend and camp onsite. A line of guesthouses near the festival venue is fully booked months ahead, with quiet and family camping now situated on the north side of the River Thames – you travel back and forth by special festival ferry. In 2007, severe summer floods meant much of the campsite areas were boggy, and a hasty rearrangement of car parks and camping fields was made just before the festival. The consensus was that they just about managed to get away with this, as the actual festival week was dry and sunny.

Personal experience of the Reading campsites is that they are packed, fill up quickly and you have a high likelihood of someone falling on your tent in the middle of the night. It's also difficult to pitch anything bigger than a small dome tent after Friday lunchtime – the available space disappears fast. The final day can be a problem as some revellers have been known to set light to their tents rather than pack them up – the smoke is suffocating.

One little-known fact about the Reading Festival is that there are free hot showers in the G4 campsite, close to Cow Lane, and there are rarely any queues – unlike on the rest of the site!

BBC Television has a strong presence at Reading (with a nod to Leeds). If you're too old to go, or can't get a ticket, you can always watch the action from the comfort of your own home.

LEEDS TODAY

The northern branch of the former Carling Weekend began in 1999 but violence and riots led to licence problems and the festival moved in 2002 to Bramham Park near Wetherby. Security was stepped up and the festival has earned a more peaceful reputation. Audiences are kinder than their Reading counterparts, with bottlings-off and heckling far less likely.

Leeds doesn't attract the same number of day trippers and media folk as Reading, and consequently Leeds fans see it as the more 'real' of the pair. This was amusingly reflected in the 2007 BBC TV coverage of both festivals. While presenters Edith Bowman and Zane Lowe held court from a futuristic studio suspended above the Reading arena, a live link-up with Colin Murray in Leeds revealed his 'studio' to be a few pallets round the back of the fence, surrounded by discarded beer cups and obscene graffiti. The 'underdog' mentality and relaxed approach of the Leeds Festival has made it a firm favourite of music fans from Scotland and the North of England who all claim it as their own.

Some 16 kilometres (10 miles) from Leeds city centre, the park and its stately home are privately owned by music fan Nick Lane-Fox, whose family has lived there for ten generations. Access to the site is via the A1, or shuttle buses from Leeds railway station.

As at Reading, campers at Leeds are allowed to light small campfires (although not bigger bonfires) in the camping area, and, if you are willing to look for it, entertainment continues pretty much round the clock. Cabaret runs until 2 a.m. and the cinema tent has showings until 3 a.m. Livelier campsites have all-night entertainment and festivalgoers even have a chance to DJ at after-parties in each of the main campsites.

LINKS
Reading
22–24 August
www.readingfestival.com
Leeds
22–24 August
www.leedsfestival.com

T in the Park

The 'T' stands, of course, for 'Tennents', the ubiquitous Scottish lager, and these days 80,000 thirsty festivalgoers get through a small loch-full of the stuff over the course of the T weekend.

Fifteen years ago, the first big Scottish festival was held in Strathclyde Country Park near Loch Lomond, and despite only 17,000 paying ticket holders turning up to see the likes of Rage Against the Machine and Björk, T in the Park became a fixture on the scene from then on in.

For the past decade the festival has been held at Balado, which is fairly easily accessible from all parts of Scotland.

Featuring a world-class line-up, the festival is aimed mainly at the young adult and student market rather than families – no children under five years of age are allowed onsite.

Away from the main stages, the festival has a funfair, silent disco and the legendary Ceilidh tent. Contrary to the outsiders' image of Scottish eating habits, the Healthy T area, launched in 2007, was a resounding success, with celebrity chefs whipping up wholesome snacks and smoothies for hungry T partygoers.

LINKS
Balado, Perth and Kinross
11–13 July
www.tinthepark.com

The Manic Street Preachers in Chelmsford in 2007

V Festival

'It was the first festival I ever went to and and I had such a awesome time I try to come back every year.'

Variously described as the five-star festival, the festival for people who don't like festivals and 'corporate hell' depending on who you talk to, V is an incredibly popular event but remains unloved compared to other leading gigs.

Targeting the same young crowd that flocks to Reading and Leeds just a week later, V, held over two days each year in twin venues in Chelmsford, Essex, and Weston Park, Staffordshire, consistently rates much lower in the NME annual poll for best festival. Yet the V festivals – which have boasted stages sponsored by Puma trainers and Strongbow cider – trade off their lack of edginess with strong line-ups of contemporary UK and international acts and at atmosphere which is safe and non-threatening.

Yes, it's extremely corporate – just check out the V-for-Virgin logo – and you're not going to feel at all subversive or part of the counterculture as a V festivalgoer. But, if it's the music that counts, with a bit of planning and organization, you can catch a large number of well-known rock and pop acts in comparative comfort over the course of the two days.

V pioneered the dual-festival concept, since taken up by Reading and Leeds, effectively doubling the festival capacity (although festivalgoers can only feasibly attend one event) and enabling the organizers to attract top headliners such as Coldplay and the Foo Fighters.

The worst punter reviews of the 2007 festivals were for the traffic queues, both getting onto the site and leaving at the end of the weekend. Many people seem to base their choice of festival on V's reputation as well organized, so when there is a slip-up such as long exit queues, they come down on the organization more harshly here than they might elsewhere.

V attracts a young crowd, and the Chelmsford VIP area especially seems be picked on by the tabloids looking for D-list celebs behaving badly.

Notable headliners include the Prodigy and surprisingly, given their anti-corporate and anti-globalization views, Radiohead, who made no secret in the music press of their dilemma about whether to play or not.

Uniquely among large festivals, a Soviet-style ticket system for the bar is in operation. First you queue to buy a token, then exchange this for your pint. Inevitably, this leads to pocketfuls of unused tokens at the end of the weekend, but you can send these off to an address on the V website to get your money back.

LINKS
Essex/Staffordshire
16–17 August
www.vfestival.com

O2 Wireless

Faithless at 02 Wireless, Leeds 2007

London gets a weekend of one-day concerts in Hyde Park but Wireless Leeds has been a proper, camping festival (for an extra £25) since 2007. The Harewood House location means there is enough room to have a full-blown festive weekend. Despite a strong line-up headed by The White Stripes, in 2007 tickets were fairly easily available close to the date.

The acts are shared between London and Leeds, with local bands also getting the chance to play. Its target market is late teens/early 20s, although accompanied children are permitted.

The music is on three stages, covering the fashionable end of Indie, alternative, and electronica. There is an ever-popular fairground as well as relaxation areas. Users of 02 mobile phones have access to their own special performance tent, with exclusive gigs, a bit more breathing space and nicer loos. The event makes up in activity what it may lack in soul.

LINKS
Harewood House, Leeds
16–17 June
www.o2wirelessfestival.co.uk

Beautiful Days

Escot Park, Devon

15–17 August

www.beautifuldays.org

Friendly, slightly crusty festival that embraces old punk bands and modern alternative folk. Great family atmosphere, but watch out for the mud!

Held in a pretty but hilly site near Exeter in Devon, Beautiful Days is the living embodiment of festival stalwarts the Levellers' ideal festival. The band founded the festival in 2003, after a career that has taken them to the world's music festivals for 20 years (and they still appear on the circuit). The Levellers traditionally perform at least twice during the weekend – once as their acoustic alter egos Drunk In Public (usually Friday night in the Big Top) and triumphantly as the main stage festival finale on Sunday evening.

With a headcount capped at 10,000, tickets sell out well ahead of the event. The festival aims to capture the old Glastonbury/Elephant Fayre vibe, and shuns corporate sponsorship and mainstream acts in favour of real ale, independent stalls and alternative and folk-based music.

What was your best ever festival and why?
Beautiful Days 2005. It restored my belief in festivals.
Sandra, Oxford

As someone once put it: 'If they've got a fiddle player, they'll be asked to play Beautiful Days.'

Many of the bands were regulars at the free festivals in the eighties and nineties, and the fans include a fair number of middle-aged former punks and squatters who are now settled with jobs, mortgage and family, but still love nothing more than firing up the camper van and reliving their youth, albeit in a safer and more comfortable environment. Expect lots of dreadlocks, fairy wings, stilt-walkers, impromptu marching bands, and armies of enthusiastic and colourfully dressed children.

In 2005, one of the festival highlights was a nightly performance of 'Freeborn John', a political history lesson with music, telling the story of John Lilburne, radical and unsung hero of the English Civil War. Performers included members of the Levellers, New Model Army and Maddie Prior of Steeleye Span. The event received a rapturous response, with standing ovations every night and is touring the UK in early 2008.

Recent headliners have included KT Tunstall, Gogol Bordello and Echo and the Bunnymen, with quality folk, comedy and rock acts competing for attention in a number of smaller tents. Legendary dance club Whirlygig set up camp in the Big Top in 2007.

Weather-wise, Beautiful Days has traditionally lived up to its name, with gorgeous August weather seemingly its birthright, which always makes the atmosphere light and the costumes colourful. That is until 2007, when the whole site fell victim to the wet weather, and the arena suffered from being ankle deep in sticky mud. Organizers seemed unable to cope with the extent of the treacherous quagmire, so if you're planning on going along, pray for fine weather, more hay bales or take the initiative and invest in a pair of waders.

What was your best ever festival and why?
Beautiful Days 2007. For some reason it all came together – great bands, great people, great food. I think a festival can be great because of what you are escaping from as well as what you are escaping to, and there was a fair amount to escape from this year. The mud didn't even spoil it.
Dave, Chichester

Belladrum Tartan Heart Festival

Belladrum Estate, Inverness, Highland, Scotland

8–9 August

www.tartanheartfestival.co.uk

Mark Treasure of Ghosts (above) and Matt Bowman of The Pigeon Detectives (below) at Belladrum 2007

This underground Highland hit near Beauly is small but perfectly formed, and for reasons best known to the organizers is chock-full of gardening metaphors and organic vegetables. Oh yes, forget Pot Noodles: at Bella you can buy fresh organic fruit and vegetables onsite. And all the stages are named in a horticultural style.

In 2007, the Garden, Grassroots, Venus Flytrap and Seedlings stages played host to the likes of Alabama 3, James and Martha Wainright, plus the usual alternative Indie and folk favourites from the Scottish and UK circuits, and 2008 promises to be in the same vein. Fancy dress is a theme, and organizers are urging people to come 'disguised in your fantasies.'

After the amplified music shuts down at night, everyone is invited to a ceilidh on the Friday night and a masked ball on the Saturday. BBC Radio Scotland broadcasts from the site and the festival fringe has grown into a

fortnight of events in the local area, culminating in the weekend of the festival itself in mid-August. Apart from the music stages, entertainment includes street theatre, the Verb Garden for poetry, comedy, debate and performance, and the Heilin' Fields for alternative therapy. You can even do a fire walk for charity.

Children under 12 are admitted free and have a wide range of activities laid on – Bella is proudly family-friendly.

Bestival

Robin Hill Country Park, Isle of Wight
5–7 September
www.bestival.net

Those in the know will single Bestival out as their favourite of all festivals. Not that this young and growing event on the Isle of Wight doesn't deserve the accolade: on the contrary it's pretty damn perfect. And therein lies the problem: if word gets out then there is danger of 'Glastonbury syndrome' setting in and Bestival becoming the festival that EVERYONE tries to get to – and then the magic is lost.

On the other hand, after 2007's triumph, which built on the success of the previous three years, it seems everybody is talking about Bestival anyway, with Channel 4 broadcasting three nights of highlights around the same time that tickets went on sale for 2008. By the time you are reading this, you will be very lucky to be able to get hold of a ticket for this year.

The advice though is, if you can, go for it. No matter what your music taste, you will find joy at Bestival. Scissor Sisters, Chemical Brothers, Beastie Boys, and loads more quality acts have performed there, as well as painfully hip breakthrough acts, such as Jack Penate and Kate Nash in 2007. Hell, even if you don't like music, you'll love the thing – just hang out in the Jestival comedy tent, the Solar Cinema 24-hour movie house, Restival chill out, the tea tent where burlesque performers serve afternoon tea all day, art installations in the woods, and the inflatable chapel where you can get 'married', should it take your fancy.

But the real difference with Bestival is that instead of grizzled old rockers and technicolour nu-ravers, you get pirates, ninjas and whole crews of ghostbusters. It's a festival in costume, and it's dressed up as the biggest fancy dress party you've ever seen. We're not talking a few eccentrics here – at least 80 per cent of the crowd are in costume and we're talking the sort that takes months of planning. Matching teams of bumblebees buzz around in a swarm, the entire cast of *Scooby Doo* drive by in a painted cardboard Mystery Machine, Fidel Castro chats away on his mobile phone, pausing only to exclaim *'Viva la revolucion!'* at passers-by.

It might be the island setting and the associated hardships of getting there (the ferry across the Solent takes a couple of hours plus queuing, and costs a fair whack for a carload of people), the fancy dress or the final-fling sense that summer's almost over, but this is by far the friendliest and most chilled-out festival you are likely to attend.

The organizer Rob da Bank, is an incredibly well-connected DJ on Radio 1 –which means he can call upon a roster of A-list and up-and-coming talent to introduce a band here, or spin tunes in a tiny tent there.

The only downside is the layout of the whole thing – the car parks are a long walk uphill which is a real downer on the Sunday night when you're carrying all your gear back to the car. The festival itself is in a long strip, with the main stage at one end, camping at the other, so however much you eat and drink, you're guaranteed a weekend of walking to work it off.

> **What was your best ever festival and why?**
> *So many to choose from, but probably Bestival in 2007. The sun shone, the crowd were great, the line-up was a great mix of old and new and the whole weekend had a real festive feel to it – not just bands playing a field, but a festival in the truest sense of the word.*
> **Jon, Winchester**

Big Chill

Eastnor Castle, Herefordshire

1–3 August

www.bigchill.net

If Glastonbury's roots are hippie, and Reading's is rock, then Big Chill is the original festival to come out of the club scene.

Since its inception as a one-day event in 1994, Big Chill has famously been somewhere for ardent clubbers to go when they retire from weekly raving – and the festival was reeling in 29,000 of them in 2007.

The Big Chill has moved around over the years, but has found its latest home at Eastnor Castle Deer Park among the Malvern Hills. The organizers boast that at Big Chill events you can expect to hear everything from classical to dance music, including folk, jazz, hip hop, world music, funk, soul, blues, pop, lounge and ambient. In 2007, New Young Pony Club, Richie Havens, The Go! Team and the year's sensation, Seasick Steve, performed.

Regulars are fiercely loyal to this, the original boutique festival, with plenty of school-age children growing up as Big Chillers almost from birth. Despite the competition from newer events offering similar laid-back thrills, Big Chill has gone from strength to strength, and is now running festival events worldwide, as well as at two permanent London venues. The festival is often spoken of in hallowed tones, as if to spread the word too much will somehow kill the magic.

So what's different about the Big Chill? It's got to be the people. While the festival showcases a wide range of dance-based sounds, and pioneered the boutique-style event with art, cabaret and multimedia happenings, other festivals have since followed suit. But the Big Chill people are determined their weekend will be special. The Big Chill Sundancers even try to influence the weather (with positive results, it seems). The festival suffers the usual woes of medium-sized events (thefts were a problem in 2007), but on the whole the event is happy, relaxed and special – a great big chill-out, in fact.

> **Top tip for first-time festivalgoers**
> *Relax, enjoy yourself, take time out to explore and talk to people rather than running screaming from set to set. It's a festie, not a military operation.*
> **Lance, Norwich**

Big Green Gathering

Cheddar, Somerset
6–10 August
www.big-green-gathering.com

If you like loud guitars and hot dogs, then Big Green Gathering is probably not for you. In fact, although the music element of this long-running festival is central to its existence, the emphasis on sustainability and organics means you are more likely to be kept up by all-night didgeridoo jams than hip hop beat boxes.

Alongside the performers, equal billing is given to the healing areas, the issue-based workshops and hands-on crafts. Children are well-catered for and there is a special teen area.

Strict policies banning Coca Cola (and most fizzy drinks) and war toys, and encouraging Fairtrade items in the marketplace, are enforced and, in keeping with the green message, all generators are banned; solar showers provide hot water, and turbines and pedal power amplify the stages.

Drug-taking and drunkenness are discouraged, and there is no bar onsite. Anyone with more than enough booze for personal consumption faces the prospect of having it confiscated.

> **What did you like about the festival?**
> I loved the variety of stalls, and different things on offer. Leon's vegetarian food was so amazing I bought his cookbook, and I loved the edible plates it was served on.
> **Gail, Loughton**

As this book went to press, the future of the Big Green Gathering was in jeopardy, as the organization was in debt. The festival scene and green businesses were rallying round with a crisis fundraising campaign well underway, but funds had only reached 20 per cent of the target. So the jury's out on whether there will be a Big Green Gathering or not in 2008. It would certainly be a great shame to see such a well-loved and unique event fall off the UK festival calendar.

Big Session

De Montfort Hall and Gardens, Leicester
13–15 June
www.bigsessionfestival.com

Brought to you by the same team that produces Summer Sundae, the Big Session is a folk festival at the De Montfort Hall and Gardens in Leicester, in its fourth year in 2008.

Folk rockers Oysterband host the event, a weekend dedicated to folky sounds in all their forms. Apart from the folk music, Big Session places great importance on children and the environment going to great lengths to both keep the little 'uns entertained and to reduce the festival's carbon footprint.

Big Session's environmental commitment came up trumps in the 2007 Festival Awards, winning the green festival prize. The venue's lack of handy car parking and city location makes it attractive to people arriving by public transport, and the recycling points are diligently used.

Children's activities are among the best at any festival, so families make up a large proportion of Big Sessioners each year, helping the Session gain its reputation as laid-back and mellow.

Holding a festival in mid-June is risky weather-wise, but until 2007 the Session enjoyed heatwaves each year. Along with so many events, 2007's Session started as a mudbath – but by the Sunday the sun was shining once again and organizers say they are prepared for any conditions in 2008.

This year is also Oysterband's 30th anniversary, so expect something a little bit special for their appearance in 2008.

Blissfields

The Matterley Bowl, Winchester, Hampshire
4–6 July
www.blissfields.co.uk

In terms of festivals, Blissfields is absolutely minuscule – attracting just 1,000 punters each year. It is a not-for-profit charity fundraiser where artists and organizers give their services for free, their ethos is to showcase new bands, and their offshoot record label and city gig nights (some with open-mic nights) continue the theme.

This teeny tiny festival in Hampshire is named after its organizers, Paul and Mel Bliss, who started the event in their (huge) back garden in 2001 simply as a bunch of friends getting together to play music. Despite its size, it's a perfectly formed festival, with camping, beer tent, a range of catering and even a second stage onsite. Eight years down the line, 2008's Blissfields will be bigger, a day longer, and held for the first time at a new venue, say the organizers, explaining that 2007's festival was 'bursting at the seams' and due to local opposition there was no chance of expanding the existing site. However, it won Best Small Festival at the 2007 UK Festival Awards.

Despite the planned capacity increase, expect Blissfields 2008 to be another early sell-out.

Bloodstock Open Air

Catton Hall, Derbyshire
15–17 August
www.bloodstock.uk.com

'Like one big happy metal family' is the excitable description by one dedicated Bloodstock fan of this small festival held in the Midlands and devoted to all music heavy and metal.

Musical diversity is not an issue at this 10,000-strong gathering, but whether you prefer your metal prefixed by thrash-, dark-, speed-, death-, doom- or goth-, Bloodstock will have a sub-genre for you.

The names Dimmu Borgir, Testament and Lacuna Coil may not be exactly household names, but if yours is a headbanging household, then the all-ages Bloodstock Open Air is festival heaven. If after 10 hours of testosterone-fuelled metal mayhem each day you find yourself needing yet more, then there's always the late-night metal karaoke back in the token bar. Running from Thursday to Saturday, Bloodstock boasts a passionate following who even have their own fan club, and a dating website, so there is no need to ever headbang alone.

Bloodstock is held each August in the grounds of a country manor house, more commonly used for equestrian events and hot-air ballooning.

Bulldog Bash

Stratford-upon-Avon, Warwickshire
7–10 August
www.bulldog-bash.co.uk

Every year, there are hundreds of bike rallies around the UK, from small pub-based gatherings to weekend-long custom shows and parties. However, only one biker party has broken through to the mainstream, and that's the Bulldog Bash. Run by the Hells Angels, who also provide security for the festival, the Bulldog attracts thousands of bikers and biker-friendly folk.

Featuring drag racing (everyone can have a go), tattoo and piercing stalls alongside the more usual festival market regulars, the Bulldog attracts headline acts of the calibre of The Damned and Status Quo, but caters for modern tastes with an all-night dance tent as well. A large indoor custom bike show provides unique spectacle and great competition. Other entertainment includes a fairground, wall of death, wrestling, wet T-shirt contests and topless bike washing.

In the spirit of bike rallies, motorcycle parking is free, with charges for cars and campervans. No drink is allowed to be brought onsite either. The bars boast an 'unlimited supply' of alcohol ...

Cambridge Folk Festival

Cambridge
31 July–3 August
www.folkfest.entadsl.com/public/ff/index.shtml

Successful for more than 40 years, the Cambridge Folk Festival is a living piece of folk music history. Organizers pride themselves in booking an eclectic range of acts and performers that loosely fit within the folky umbrella, which is flexible enough to accommodate music both traditional and contemporary, ranging from gospel to country, blues, jazz, the occasional pop star and a regular ceilidh.

Unusual features of Cambridge are the tented arenas stages, the two separate campsites where you have to pre-book and pay according to the

The Chieftains performed at Cambridge in 2006

size of your tent, and the toilets, which are actually clean and comfortable. Cambridge has built up a reputation as welcoming and accessible for disabled festival fans, and families are exceptionally well catered for. There is even a crêche.

Although Cambridge attracts folk stars of the calibre of Emmylou Harris and Nick Cave, some of the best fun is to be had in the livelier Cherry Hinton Hall campsite, where impromptu sessions often run all night.

Castlepalooza

Charleville Castle Estate, County Offaly, Ireland
29–31 August
www.castlepalooza.com

No kids at this event, which is otherwise like a pocket version of Electric Picnic (see page 58) – with added class. Held over the August bank holiday weekend, Castlepalooza is not only in the grounds of a castle, it takes over the inside as well. The festival is almost unknown outside Ireland.

Independently run, the capacity is only 1,500 and it's all strictly for over-18s. The intimate size means it's possible to offer proper indoor toilets and hot showers to festivalgoers.

It's not a festival for big name acts (although 2007 saw eighties pop act Sister Sledge headlining): the music tends towards the new and raw – Castlepalooza sets itself up as something a bit different. Expect about 40 bands in 2008, across two stages, plus art exhibitions, surprise performances and a mini-cinema in the castle with cheesy movies, cushions to sit on and free chocolate and popcorn.

Connect

Inverary Castle, Argyll, Scotland
29–31 August
www.connectmusicfestival.com

Bridging the gap between the massive T in the Park and the bijou Wickerman, Connect was one of Scotland's new festivals in 2007, and marred by terrible weather. Despite this, almost immediately afterwards organizers announced that it would be returning with a bigger event in 2008 even though they'd lost money first-time around.

The setting – between a castle and a loch – is quintessentially Scottish (complete with midges), and the music showcases Scottish talent (The Jesus and Mary Chain, Primal Scream and Teenage Fanclub all featured prominently in 2007) among the general run of festival bands of the moment.

Reviews almost universally applaud the mellow, intimate vibe and lack of the idiot element that can mar so many of the bigger events.

Catering is the usual festival food plus some special one-offs – the porridge and stovies stalls offer up favourite Scottish fare, while the local oysters on sale reflect the 'classy' atmosphere the grown-up crowd (no small kids allowed) love it for.

Top: Björk performing at the 2007 concert
Left: M.I.A. in action at Connect

Creamfields

Daresbury Estate, Halton, Cheshire
23 August
www.creamfieldsfestival.co.uk

The original one-day mega-rave, Creamfields is organized by Liverpool club Cream, and runs from noon until late into the night, with dance music of all persuasions thumping from a number of marquees and stages – and skate ramps and displays to give people something to look at.

No camping, and everyone has to go home at dawn, but apart from that, Creamfields has many of the elements of a 'proper' festival – food outlets, a fantastic market, and a 10-hour live broadcast on Radio One.

Definitely not child-friendly and appealing to a young adult crowd, Creamfields is a glow-stick paradise after dark when things get moving.

Croissant Neuf Summer Party

Usk, Monmouthshire, Wales
15–17 August
www.partyneuf.co.uk

First held in 2007, this entirely solar-powered festival near Usk in Monmouthshire is organized by the same people who have brought the Croissant Neuf Circus tent to dozens of festivals over the past 20-odd years.

A low-key event, and very child-friendly, here is a strong focus on alternative healing and renewable energy. The food and drink is all organic.

Apart from acts on the main stage, much of the entertainment is seemingly spontaneous and mobile, and culminates in a dress-up Masked Ball involving everyone.

Download Festival

See Major Festivals pages 30–31

Electric Picnic

Stradbelly Hall, County Laois, Ireland
29–31 August
www.electricpicnic.ie

Founded in 2004, Electric Picnic is Ireland's successful take on the medium-sized boutique festival. Held in the picturesque Stradbally Hall Estate, the event has grown in just a few years from a one-day affair to a full-blown three-day festival, which sells out well in advance.

Picnickers return each year for the top-class eclectic line-up along with a feeling of openness and space unusual for a sold-out festival. Easily reached from both Dublin and Kildare, the 32,500-capacity festival also has its share of fans who cross the Irish Sea for the weekend.

Bands come from both the cutting-edge of music and the back catalogues, with an emphasis on alternative superstars. The line-up for 2007's included The Stooges, The Undertones, Polyphonic Spree and Patrick Wolf.

Onsite is a comedy tent, kids area, healing area, silent disco, cinema, a fairy lounge hosted by Fairy Love fairies and most of Glastonbury's Lost Vagueness field complete with inflatable chapel. Under-12s are admitted free and there is children's entertainment, but 12- to 17-year-olds are not admitted as the festival is 'still being developed [and] it isn't completely child friendly'.

Glastonbury

See Major Festivals pages 18–29

Glastonwick

Coombes, West Sussex
4–6 July
www.cask-ale.co.uk/beerfestival.html

Founded in 1996 by punk poet Attila the Stockbroker, Glastonwick is 'three days of real ale, real music and real poetry'.

'Having been to loads of beer festivals with crap music, and loads of music festivals with crap beer, we decided to organize one where the beer was as good as the music (and vice versa) with very popular results'.

All bands and performers booked for Glastonwick are basically friends of Attila, who comperes the event. Beer lovers are well-catered for with about 65 cask-conditioned ales, all from small independent breweries and 10 farmhouse ciders and perries available.

Children are welcome, and although there is no entertainment specifically aimed at them, it's rumoured that tractor rides have been organized on occasion.

Global Gathering

Long Marston Airfield, Stratford-upon-Avon, Warwickshire

25–26 July

www.globalgathering.co.uk

A dance party that has grown into a festival by default (it's really two one-day events spliced together, with an adjacent campsite), Global Gathering is now the UK's biggest dance festival. A stellar line-up of DJs is the main attraction, although the open-air cinema, adrenaline village for thrill fans, and the occasional fly-past by the Red Arrows adds to the party atmosphere. It is often overlooked by mainstream festival fans, but this West Midlands event has a true global, if specialized, appeal.

Greenbelt

Cheltenham Racecourse, Gloucestershire

22–25 August

www.greenbelt.org.uk

Greenbelt is possibly unique, in both the secular and Christian arenas. Certainly in the UK, there just isn't anything else like it at all. Although it was born as a Christian music festival, the remit these days is very wide.

There's art and music of just about every kind, as well as a comprehensive seminar programme. By no means all of the speakers and artists are Christians – some of them are secular or of other faiths, but share Greenbelt's ethos of social justice and a celebration of the arts and creation. Some aspects of the programme are explicitly Christian, but a lot of it isn't, and there's certainly no 'in-your-face' preaching.

Greenbelt's content is often regarded as controversial by more traditional Christians, and this is what makes so many people love it so much. It's an event that will really make you think. The programme these days is extremely diverse, with truly something for everyone.

Unusually in Christian circles, Greenbelt has an inclusive and welcoming attitude to gay people, and runs events for them with no agenda.

This is a very family-orientated festival, offering a safe space for children, and free from the usual excesses associated with drink and drugs. However, even Greenbelt-goers acknowledge that it's quite suburban and middle class.

Green Man

Glanusk Park, Brecon Beacons, Wales
15–17 August
www.thegreenmanfestival.co.uk

This could win the title of the hairiest festival in the UK. The number of beards is astonishing – until you realize the line-up is strongly in favour of folk and blues, neither of which are known for their clean-cut followers. Last year's headliner Robert Plant was by far the biggest name, but there are other delights to take in, including knitting workshops and demonstrations of water dowsing.

Small and independent, Green Man is a bit different, eccentric even. Everything's on a human scale, and even when the crowd swells to 15,000, it's still fairly easy to shift from stage to stage. Some people think it's getting too big – only four years ago there were 345 people present.

A long way from anywhere in the Brecon Beacons, it's reassuring to know that home comforts are important at Green Man. The toilets are clean, comfortable and stocked with loo roll and hand-wash for the full weekend. Quite literally a breath of fresh air in the Welsh countryside.

Guilfest

Stoke Park, Guildford,
Surrey
6–8 July
www.guilfest.co.uk

Formerly the Guildford Festival of Folk and Blues, Guilfest has been running since 1992 and these days its music policy covers rock, pop, alternative and big names from the eighties and nineties.

Stoke Park is a town-centre park with manicured grass and a level setting – ideal for wheelchair-users and families. Although the festival is popular each year with campers, many of the ticket-holders come on day tickets, so the campsite is small enough to avoid the whole 'festival trudge' at the end of the night back to the tents.

BBC Radio 2 broadcasts from the festival, and the line-up seems to appeal equally to teenagers and their middle-aged parents. Headliners in 2007 included Supergrass, Squeeze and Toots and the Maytals. With two main stages, a cabaret tent, unsigned bands stage, a secure kids' area and a dance tent, as well as a large market, food village and healing area, there are lots of events happening all the time.

In 2007, Saturday morning's wake-up call was from the Guildford Philharmonic Orchestra on the main stage – an unusual hangover cure.

With so many day visitors and a leisure centre opposite offering hot showers and swimming, it's one of the cleanest festivals around and an ideal taster festival for first-timers.

The Ordinary Boys on stage at Guilford 2007

Isle of Wight
See Major Festivals page 32

Latitude

Southwold, Suffolk
17–20 July
www.latitudefestival.com

This festival thinks it's clever – and it's probably right. Latitude is put together by the same team that produces much of Glastonbury. This is their boutique event.

Marcus Brigstocke in the Latitude comedy arena

The music element, over four stages, can't be faulted for its demographic – thirty-something families who have graduated from the mainstream monster festivals and are looking for something friendlier and smaller.

The literary arena hosts a weekend-full of book readings, famous author appearances, discussions and forums. The cabaret arena offers both titillation and torture, as well as interactive areas. The theatre arena is like a mini Edinburgh Fringe, with previews of many shows heading to Edinburgh later in the summer. In the poetry arena, there's everything from storytelling to hip hop, slam poets, bizarre raconteurs and spoken word performances. Add to all this a comedy arena, an area combining music and film, plus a host of hidden parties in the woods, and you get the feel for the broad ranging appeal of Latitude.

It's fiercely family-friendly and even nice to day-ticket holders who can't get home, with a special day-ticket holders' overnight campsite.

Singer-songwriter José González performed in 2006

Leeds

See Major Festivals pages 34–39

Loopallu

Ullapool (shores of Loch Broom), Highland, Scotland
19–20 September
www.loopallu.co.uk

With a 2007 line-up featuring spiky art rockers Franz Ferdinand and the Ullapool Pipe Band, you know you're getting something different at the 3,000-capacity Loopallu.

Quite literally turning its host village on its head, Loopallu doubles the population of Ullapool each year. Its remote location doesn't put off the thousands who ensure the festival is a fast sell-out. Loopallu has a knack for attracting both major and breakthrough bands, and people travel from all over the world to attend. On the fringe, the whole of Ullapool joins in the festival spirit. Local pubs host bands, there's street entertainment and according to *The Scotsman* they serve 'the classiest festival food ever seen'.

O2 Wireless Festival
See Major Festivals page 43

Oxegen
See Major Festivals page 33

Reading
See Major Festivals pages 34–39

Rockness

Loch Ness, Dores, near Inverness, Scotland
7–8 June
www.rockness.co.uk

As the name suggests, this newish festival rocks the banks of spooky Loch Ness in the north of Scotland.

Bookmakers William Hill even handed out 50,000 disposable cameras in 2007 in a challenge to festivalgoers to snap the elusive Loch Ness Monster, presumably on the off-chance that the sounds of Daft Punk would lure him from the depths to take a peek. As no earth-shattering images were subsequently revealed, it can be safely assumed that the cameras were mainly used to take bad photos of crowds, tents, random bright lights and gleeful kilt-raising Scotsmen. But as the festival takes place on what organizers describe as the most beautiful festival site in the world, there would be no shortage of scenic shots to be had.

With a 35,000 capacity, Rock Ness is a feast of world-class acts in a corner of the UK normally starved of decent gigs. This festival already has all the trimmings: four stages showcasing 70 bands, dance tents, cinema, 24-hour food, themed bars and luxury camping.

Acts for 2008 hadn't been confirmed as this book went to press, but the organizers promise it's the only festival with its own monster – whether he makes an appearance or not!

Stonehenge Solstice Celebration

Stonehenge, Wiltshire
20–21 June
www.newage.co.uk

Not strictly meeting the criteria for this guide (there's no camping onsite and the entire event is completed within 12 hours or so), it still would be a huge mistake to miss out Stonehenge.

Designed to align with the rising sun at the solstice, Stonehenge was erected between 3000 BC and 1600 BC. It has been a focal point of midsummer celebrations by many cultures ever since, and in the hippy era a large, anarchistic, drug-fuelled free festival was held onsite, featuring bands as diverse as Dexys Midnight Runners and Hawkwind.

After the original Stonehenge Free Festival was banned in 1984, a court and police clampdown meant that the stones were off-limits for several years to everyone but selected Druids at the time of the summer solstice.

These days, restrictions have relaxed enough to allow a sort of free festival to take place among the stones, although access is restricted to a late-night arrival the night before and an early getaway on midsummer's morning. Car parking is 1.6 kilometres (1 mile) away from the site itself and no shelters of any kind can be erected. No amplified music is allowed onsite, although the dozens of drummers, whistleblowers and revellers turn the event into an all-night party. The upside of the strict organization is that there is little if any trouble and there are plenty of clean toilets as well as hot food and drink stalls available.

According to *Festival Eye* magazine, discussions are ongoing with English Heritage to allow more music on a special stage to one side to make the experience less focused on the stones themselves.

Strummercamp

Ashton-under-Lyne, Manchester

May bank holiday

www.strummercamp.co.uk

A free festival in Manchester in tribute to the late Clash frontman Joe Strummer – as random as is sounds, it has actually come good, with two years now under the organizers' belts and a third planned for 2008.

Featuring a mixture of Clash tribute bands, punk acts and contemporaries of Strummer himself, Strummercamp is underground and proud. A thin website, with little real information given away, belies the popularity of this specialized event for those who want to keep Joe Strummer's legacy alive.

Attracting name bands alongside the copyists, Strummercamp is something of a pilgrimage for Clash fans everywhere, and Manchester Rugby Club, although an unlikely venue, seems to keep everyone happy.

Summer Sundae Weekender

De Montfort Hall, Leicester

8–10 August

www.summersundae.com

Leicester manages to pull off that rare feat – an urban festival with a greenfield feel. SSW is in its eighth year and has grown from a regional, day event to a three-day festival with a national profile and a reputation for family-friendliness – while keeping numbers restricted to just 6,000.

Centred on the city's De Montfort Hall and spilling out into its grounds, SSW has five stages – the main stage in the hall itself, one outdoor arena and three marquees. There is also a 'secret' stage, the Hub, where the lucky few catch intimate acoustic sets from bands appearing at the festival. A benefit of the venue is the use of its 2,000-capacity auditorium, and all the associated bars, flushing toilets, staff, and technical facilities already onsite.

Music-wise, the booking policy is to be as wide-ranging as possible to encourage ticket-holders to open their ears to new sounds. One stage is dedicated to up-and-coming acts, another is programmed by *Musician* magazine, while the indoor and outdoor main stages showcase the biggest bands – the likes of Patti Smith, Sophie Ellis-Bextor and KT Tunstall have all performed at the Weekender.

A big top in the festival village serves as the cabaret stage, with comedy and entertainers in a bill put together by Leicester Comedy Festival. Finally the kids' area is weatherproof and indoors, with a full programme of activities from breakfast time to bedtime stories.

There are two separate campsites adjacent to the festival itself. Being so close to the centre of Leicester, there are plenty of fringe events running simultaneously in town and buses run regularly from both campsites to the fringe venues. Parking is limited and difficult, however. There are special arrangements with nearby NCP car parks, but at an average charge of £4.50 a day, the costs soon mount up.

T in the Park

See Major Festivals pages 40–41

Bragg on stage

Tolpuddle Martyrs Festival

Tolpuddle, Dorset
12–13 July
www.tolpuddlemartyrs.org.uk

If one thing is for sure, it's that Tolpuddle isn't for everyone. If you're a raver, headbanger, Top 40 or rap fan, then it won't appeal.

It's certainly no alternative for Guilfest, which runs the same weekend most years, if you're looking for a full-on festival experience. It's not for you if you think folk music is old hat, hate unions and 'good causes' or if you think Margaret Thatcher was a great leader for this country.

The Tolpuddle Martyrs Festival grew out of the annual trade union rally at the Dorset village, commemorating the lives of the six agricultural labourers who were convicted in 1834 for forming a then-illegal union.

Over the years, the festival has grown from a one-day affair to a weekend of music, spoken word and activism. The event is free, except for camping and car parking, and takes place on the lawn in front of the Martyrs Museum and in adjacent fields. If village fêtes were organized by trade unions, they would all be like Tolpuddle.

For a small event with a fête-like atmosphere, Tolpuddle has attracted some notable bands. Billy Bragg plays each year to a rapturous crowd, and 2007 saw The Men They Couldn't Hang and Chumbawamba performing live, with folk and comedy vying with speeches in the daytime and comedy and a dance tent running on the Saturday night.

Truck Festival

Steventon, Oxfordshire
5–6 July
www.thisistruck.com

Oxfordshire's Truck Festival is a deliberately small, anti-commercial event, with a sell-out capacity of around 4,000. The festival is part of a welcome trend towards informal festivals around the country. Celebrating its 11th year in 2008, Truck organizers are happy that their festival flies beneath the radar of the popular press and retains its family feel.

The people behind Truck are music fans, who one day thought it would be a great idea to hold a festival of their own on a working farm in their own village of Steventon. Truck is a real village event, with the local church selling ice cream, breakfasts served up by the local Rotary Club, and local bands making up the bulk of the line-up. There was even a family quilt put together by Truck fans for the 10th anniversary. All proceeds each year go to charity – more than £200,000 to date.

Incidentally, although the festival's main stage is built upon three flatbed trucks, that's not how the festival got its name. Founder Robin Bennett chose the name after picking up a CD titled *Ten Trucking Greats* and also liked the connection with the great sixties slogan 'Keep on Truckin'.

Fans of Truck Festival are a loyal bunch and its one of the safest festivals around. Although it's always a sell-out, latecomers can usually pick up spare tickets for less than face value near the dates on the festival forum.

When the floods of July 2007 left the area knee-deep in water, the festival was cancelled at literally the eleventh hour. When organizers rescheduled the event for two months later, they were able to keep almost the same line-up and resume where they'd left off, to a capacity crowd and much goodwill, this time in glorious sunshine.

Despite its diminutive size, Truck Festival boasts six stages, from the outdoor main stage to the Barn, which shift from punky live acts in the daytime to after-hours raving, all the while smelling of the cows that have temporarily loaned out their home.

V Festival
See Major Festivals pages 41–43

Wickerman

Kirkcarswell Farm, near Kirkcudbright, Galloway, Scotland
25–26 July
www.thewickermanfestival.co.uk

Scotland's original boutique festival, Wickerman is named after the 10-metre (30-foot) wicker sculpture that dominates the site and is burned as a sacrifice on the Saturday night.

Only 10,000 tickets go on sale (many are sold the year before as early bird specials), but the festival has more music than anyone could get round in one weekend – 11 stages across the 48-hectare (120-acre) site.

As well as the main stages (named Woodward and Summerisle – yes expect references to the *The Wicker Man* movie), there is a world music and funk tent, Eden zone, a classic Jamaican reggae sound system, acoustic village, scooter tent, children's area, workshops, beer tent and crafts. The line-up favours old punk bands although the musical range is pretty eclectic and there are a lot of young families around, especially in the daytime.

The Woodward stage is unique – made from 12-metre (40-foot) larch trees chained and tethered into a dome. Bands that have played this stage include The Damned, The Buzzcocks and Alabama 3.

Everything stops for the big Wickerman burning at midnight on Saturday, but for the rest of the time it's wall-to-wall music with major acts alternating between the twin main stages.

Scotland absolutely loves this little festival down in the south-west – tickets are extremely hot and reviews are almost all five-star.

3 Wishes Faery Fest

Bodmin Moor, Cornwall
20–22 June
www.3wishesfaeryfest.co.uk

This gathering of the self-proclaimed faery clans is held on Bodmin Moor for 'three fairytastic days' at midsummer.

Not the type of festival that attracts gangs of beer-swilling lads, Faery Fest is bursting with female energy. Its publicity describes it as family-friendly and a place 'where humans and faerie folk can walk (or fly!) side-by-side in harmony, in celebration of the magical time of midsummer. The faery ring is opening at this time, a midsummer's gateway into the realms of fae, an opportunity to glimpse into fairyland, and to experience how the '"little people" celebrate their love of the sacred land'.

The line-up in 2007 was headed by The Mediaeval Baebes, with a strong pagan, Celtic folk rock influence amongst the performers, many of whom appeared in full fairy costume. Of course, this made them look exactly like the audience, who are all fairies too. Anyone mistakenly turning up in human costume could quickly rectify this by stopping by the faery craft market, selling 'clothes, headdresses, wings, wands, arts and other fairy goodies and gifts'.

Performances to look out for include a magical midsummer faery masquerade and procession, dancing fire faeries, goblin drummers, wing and wand making workshops, and a faery fashion show!

Faery Fest has a range of ticket options, the larger your group, the more you save. All tickets include camping onsite (what do fairies sleep in?).

WOMAD

Malmesbury, Wiltshire
25–27 July
http://womad.org

BIG RED
TENT

LITTLE
BIG TOP

SKATE
ARENA

The WOMAD (World of Music, Arts and Dance) organization has been promoting world music festivals since the early 1980s, when events were overseen by leading light Peter Gabriel. Over 25 years, the WOMAD brand has grown so that its festivals now take place in the UK and other countries including Australia, New Zealand, Singapore, Holland and Spain.

In 2007, the UK WOMAD festival left its site in Reading and moved to Wiltshire, where up to 80,000 people turned up for a long weekend of world beats, great market stalls, amazing global food choices and plenty of entertainment for kids, including that rarest of things, a proper crèche, where children spend time building props and making costumes for the now traditional Sunday lunchtime parade.

Bright, rootsy, green and clean by festival standards, WOMAD is a perfect family festival. Be prepared to enjoy some of the world's finest reggae, salsa, hi-life, blues, folk, raï, bhangra, jazz, hip-hop, koto, klezmer and so on.

What was your best ever festival?

The old WOMAD festival in Reading with a big group of friends. The music was varied, not always my kind of thing, but the occasion was fantastic, better than expected as things had moved on a lot from the jazz festivals I went to in the seventies. There were great market and food stalls, second stages, late night DJ sessions and a great sense of freedom from the grimness of working in an office. I remember the rainy Monday morning at the end of my first WOMAD – the food stalls were giving away unsold stock and I drove home with hundreds of bread rolls, veggie sausages and burgers, counting down to the next festival.
Jon, Winchester

Good causes

Festivals no longer represent a cheap weekend away, but with rising prices all round it's comforting to know that not every pound from your pocket is going to be banked as profit.

Practically every festival supports at least one charity, whether by direct donation, collections onsite, employing charity volunteers to help run the event, or by donating stall space to organizations. The student steward in the hi-visibility jacket who helps you get parked could well be a volunteer. Many festivals hire in stewards through charities such as Oxfam, which makes money while offering volunteers free tickets, secure camping and generous time off over the weekend.

The cheerful ladies wandering through Bestival selling huge sunflowers to everyone who will buy one are as much a part of the festival as the bands are – and they are raising thousands of pounds for a local hospice.

After-hours entertainment at Reading and Leeds is provided by DJs working with the charity ActionAid, pushing a strong HIV warning along with their sounds.

Glastonbury, which works with large charities each year and raises money for them in a variety of ways, also shares the profits around community causes and lesser-known charities. Recently, it was announced that £74,000 was going to Banana Link, which works with trade unions in Latin America to negotiate a fair price for banana crops.

Even the smallest festivals can be charity fundraisers. Tiny Blissfields sent £2,000 to Africa in 2007 to help Practical Action, which supplies tools to local communities, as well as donating £500 to a local primary school in Hampshire.

festivals lite

What if, at the end of the day, the call of your own bed is just too strong? What you need is a festival lite.

Hyde Park Calling in London is a two-day mini-festival, with three stages and the usual food and merchandise stalls you'd expect at any proper festival. But when the music's over for the night, you just hop on a tube train or bus and creep home. Maybe it's something about Londoners, but the mini-festival-then-home-to-bed is incredibly popular, including O2's Wireless, Clapham Common's Get Loaded in the Park, and the Underage Festival, where you have to be aged 14–17 to get in – and no exceptions!

It's not all about London though. The good news is that you can find a mini-festival in just about every part of the country, where you can enjoy some of the atmosphere of the real thing without compromising on your comfort. Newcastle's Evolution Festival and Birmingham's own Soundstation Festival are just two of the one-day urban music festivals.

Most local authorities now lay on some sort of annual festival, often on bank holiday weekends, so everyone has an opportunity to sample a taste of the festival experience in their own town.

For a very small taster of some of the best city festivals, check out the events that follow.

Events such as the Hat Fair in Winchester, Hampshire, held on the weekend after Glastonbury each year and attracting many of that festival's fringe performers, is Britain's biggest street theatre festival. Taking over public spaces in the city centre, the Hat Fair encompasses circus, music, cabaret and the bizarre and takes its name from the way performers are paid – by passing a hat around.

Stokefest, in Hackney's Clissold Park in London, is a one-day free festival that turns the urban environment into a huge party. Several stages and a packed programme cover all different types of music and community-based entertainment in the course of an afternoon in early June.

Also in London, the Innocent Village Fête, which first appeared in 2007, was held in Regent's Park. The company took their village fête concept to several festivals during the summer, including Bestival on the Isle of Wight.

Coventry's Godiva free festival, held in mid-July, boasts a quality music line-up of retro and new bands, kids' entertainment and, umm … a dog show.

Liverpool's Mathew Street Festival, held in pubs, clubs and street venues around the legendary Cavern Club site, is the biggest free music festival in the world, attracting up to 350,000 people over August bank holiday weekend. Provisional dates have been announced for 2008 at the time of going to press, despite 2007's festival being curtailed due to major roadworks in the city centre.

Big in Falkirk (early May) is Scotland's national street arts festival, and is mostly free. With most events located in Callendar Park in the city, it features spectacular outdoor theatre, pyrotechnic displays, art, comedy and big name music acts.

LINKS

All Tomorrow's Parties www.atpfestival.com

Big in Falkirk www.biginfalkirk.com

Concrete Jungle
http://jacktheladproductions.com/cj2008

Evolution Festival www.evolutionfestival.co.uk

Godiva Festival www.godivafestival.co.uk

Hyde Park Calling www.hydeparkcalling.co.uk

Mathew Street Festival
http://mathewstreetfestival.co.uk

Soundstation Festival www.sound-station.co.uk

Speedfreaks Ball www.speedfreaks-ball.co.uk

Stokefest www.stokefest.co.uk

Winchester Hat Fair www.hatfair.co.uk

Camping

Staying out for the summer

For everyone's sake, remember where you pitched your tent. Look out for landmarks nearby or better still hoist your own tent flag. It's not big or clever to stumble through a sleeping campsite at 5 a.m., hollering for your lost friends.

So, you're going to a festival for the weekend. And it's too far to pop home each night. (Sleeping at home is fine if you like hot baths and clean hair; but not if you're into all-night dance tents and the 5 a.m. sunrise vibe.)

The most obvious solution to staying onsite is a tent. The rule of thumb for tents is, however many 'men' it says it accommodates, divide that by two if you want a weekend in reasonable comfort. Therefore a two-man will sleep you alone, or with a VERY close friend, but probably not his/her stuff as well. A three-man will be a tight squeeze for a couple and an eight-man ideal for a group of four friends who are looking at hosting a bit of an after party in the campsite.

Looking back at footage of festivals even 10 years ago, this is where you see one of the biggest changes in recent years. Back then, it was all two-pole pup tents with the odd bit of camouflage netting holding together little 'villages' – gazebos and domes were few and far between.

Now, though, a typical campsite will be mostly made up of lightweight dome tents of all sizes, interspersed with gazebos under which you'll find groups of friends cooking up barbecues or drinking beer and playing loud CDs of their favourite bands – often with scant regard to the sort of music actually being performed at the festival. Pop-up tents, which are erected in seconds but take the uninitiated hours to compress down again, remain popular, but the fashion tents – Cath Kidston-style designs, neo-hippy florals and even cowboy-and-Indian-style fake toy tepees are proving the fashion of the season. Whatever they're like to sleep in, for some folks the fact they can buy wellies, a kagoule and sleeping bag to match may be more important.

Camping in style

If the challenge of turning a bag of fabric and plastic poles into living accommodation is all too much, check out the local B&Bs.

This works for festivals like Reading or Leeds, where there is civilization just outside the festival perimeter. But at rural festivals such as Glastonbury, getting off- and onsite each night is just not practical. The result is the growth of super-camping options or, as someone described it in the middle of a mud-filled festival weekend, 'pretend camping for rich softies'.

For various fees, usually at least twice the price of your admission ticket, some festivals offer a range of 'extra' accommodation types, which are strictly limited in numbers and organized by third parties.

Fancy yourself as a Saharan nomad? No problem. Bedouin tents are now readily available at most festivals, erected for you and fully furnished with tasteful couches, rugs and drapes. Yearning to be a Native American chief?

How? Your tribe can stay in a tepee in a dedicated tepee village, if you're quick off the mark (tents are always oversubscribed) and have a few hundred pounds to spare on top of your ticket price.

Other special options include converted double-decker buses, beach huts, podpads (which are the size of tents but with a rigid shell), nomad yurts and retro-style American trailers. Many can be luxuriously furnished at extra cost and all are situated in special campsites with extra security and their own facilities.

At Glastonbury, one company offers luxury and not-so-posh caravans just offsite, along with furnished jousting tents, a jeep taxi to the gate and for the seriously rich, a helicopter shuttle service from Bristol. Stay there and you'll be away from the general festival buzz but potentially camping among bands and record company bosses, if that sort of thing appeals.

> **Top tip for first-time festivalgoers**
> Take plenty cash and conceal it in various places about your person. [Ideally] do not take credit cards, driving licence or anything else you can't afford to lose permanently. Crime is not the problem so much as just stuff wandering.
> **Lance, Norwich**

If your budget doesn't stretch beyond a tent, there are very nice people who will provide the tent, pitch it and take it down at the end of the weekend for you. They are called Tangerine Fields and all you have to do is pay your money and turn up. They can also organize gazebos, stoves, airbeds, sleeping bags and even caravans at some festivals. The coolest thing is that all sleeping bags are donated to the homeless charity CRISIS at the end of each festival.

New for the 2008 season is MyHab, an award-winning design by 23-year-old James Dunlop, who came up with the bright idea of a waterproof cardboard shelter after hearing about the large number of abandoned tents after festivals. 'People use and abuse their tents because they are so cheap', he said. 'They are just tired and want to go home after festivals. They don't want to mess about putting their tent away'. Watch out for MyHab alternatives to tents at festivals this year.

LINKS

www.boutiquecamping.net
www.busbeds.com
www.festivalbeachhuts.com
www.flyglastonbury.com
www.myhab.com
www.podpads.com
www.tangerinefields.co.uk

Going mobile

'Well I'm gonna find a home on wheels, see how it feels.'
Going Mobile, Pete Townshend, The Who

If you're looking for a comfort camping option, but prefer to mix with the regular festivalgoers, then a campervan could be the answer for you.

Secure, cosy, comfortable, and with no setting up (unless you bring an awning), all sorts of live-in vehicles can be seen at festivals – from the archetypal 'crusty' bus or truck, generally done up to look like something between a Romany caravan and an army truck, to massive, palatial, Six Million Dollar Man-style American RVs.

But with caravans banned from most festival sites, the classic and most popular live-in festival vehicle is of course the humble Volkswagen. From lovingly restored 1950s split-screen buses with chrome and pastel paint jobs, through seventies bay window pop-tops in Day-Glo paint, to rusty white eighties models, housing large families, and surrounded by the persistent aroma of a non-stop barbecue, VW campervans find their natural home at festivals.

Campervan fields are a world of their own, separate from the tent cities, the priorities being level parking (if that's impossible you need to be able to sleep with your head higher then your feet for a good night's sleep), awning space and somewhere to empty the Porta Potti.

Campervan field regulars are a friendly bunch, although because you are in a vehicle, you won't be forced to listen to every movement of the people next door as you are when separated by two thin pieces of nylon tent.

Mutual curiosity and admiration of each other's vehicles is the norm, as is getting together around charcoal burners for evening parties (in fact, surprisingly often you'll find that some campervanners prefer the surroundings of their own vehicle to actually watching headline acts), and on Monday mornings the sight of vans being jump-started by helpful total strangers is far from unusual.

However, don't be tempted to stick a mattress in the back of a Transit and buy a campervan pass – usually these fields are reserved for vehicles with fixed beds and sinks.

If that all sounds tempting, you can buy into the campervan dream for as little as two grand, or pay up to £20,000 for a decently restored splittie (classic VW with split screen).

If you're just dipping your toe in the van experience, you can always rent, if you get booked up early enough in the season. There are a growing number of hire firms catering specifically to the festival market, and if you go to enough festivals you will spot the same vans with different occupants at events throughout the summer. Some firms will even deliver vans to the site, so you can just transfer your gear from your car when you get there.

LINKS

www.kamperhire.co.uk

www.coolcampervans.com

www.completecaravanservices.co.uk

Camping tips

- Try to pitch your tent before dark, for obvious reasons.
- If you arrive early in a group, don't leave too much room between your tents or your may get back later to find interlopers taking up your communal party space.
- If you pitch close to pathways your tent might get trampled or tripped over and you will probably be disturbed all night.
- Camping directly under floodlights can leave the occupants silhouetted at night – think about it!
- Pitching near the toilets may seem convenient but a day into the festival they are going to stink like your worst nightmare.
- Make friends with your neighbours – you can keep an eye on each other's tents.
- Don't keep valuables in the tent.
- Don't padlock your tent, it draws the attention of tent thieves, many of whom are equipped with Stanley knifes to slash their way in anyway.
- Don't leave your tent behind on the last day, or if you do, at least pack it away and hand it to a steward – many festivals give abandoned tents to charity.

LINKS

Blacks www.blacks.co.uk

Millets www.millets.co.uk

Cheap Tents www.cheaptents.com

Freecycle http://freecycle.org

Joe Bananas www.joe-bananas.com

Camping on the cheap

Face it, the ticket itself nearly broke the bank, didn't it? And the less money you spend on camping the more there is left for beer. So just how cheaply can you get yourself set up?

The absolute minimum kit you need is a sleeping bag and a tent, and if you want to make or keep friends, a change of clothes. Ask around before you go – you'll be surprised how many people have camping gear stowed away in lofts and sheds, unused. Or try Freecycle for unwanted free stuff.

But even if you can't beg or borrow a tent for the weekend, it needn't cost a bomb to get sorted. You can pick up a roomy two-man tent out of season at Millets for around £20 and Blacks do a quality two-man tent, two sleeping bags and mats for less than £50. Argos do occasional festival specials for less than £30 – for that you get a dome tent, two sleeping mats and two sleeping bags. And at the end of the 2007 season, supermarkets were offering six-person dome tents for £50.

But if the unthinkable happens and you find yourself onsite without any kit, there are several options.

• Make friends quickly – a bit dodgy this one. You could either sort yourself out a billet for the weekend or be escorted offsite for stalking before it even gets underway.

• Throw yourself on the mercy of festival welfare – these kindly people are there for the casualties, the lost and the incapable like yourself, and may be able to fix you up with a blanket to take the edge off.

• Take credit cards and cash (but wear a body belt): most festivals these days have onsite camping stalls that can sort you out with anything from a simple blanket to a tent, bedding, lanterns, personal urinal and folding chairs. Check out Joe Bananas – once famous in festival circles as a blanket stall that played groovy music all night long, it's now the last word in emergency and pre-ordered festival camping requisites.

OTHER USEFUL CAMPING ITEMS TO BRING

- **Mallet** – to get those tent pegs into the ground if it's been a dry summer.
- **Roll-up sleeping mat** – for extra warmth and comfort and without the fuss of a blow-up mattress.
- **Torch** – especially a head-torch (from Millets or Blacks). This keeps your hands free as you wobble back to your tent late at night with your beers.
- **Water container** – even a half-litre drinking water bottle. Keep it topped-up for early-morning thirst crises.
- **Penknife** (Swiss Army-style or multi-tool).
- **Disposable barbecue** – even if you're not planning to cook, these are cheap, light to carry and can simulate a cosy campfire now that most festivals have banned open fires altogether. Don't forget to keep it away from tents though and preferably off the ground.
- **Matches or a lighter.**
- **Lantern** – either gas, battery or tea-light powered.
- **Spare batteries.**
- **The ubiquitous wet wipes.**

Green issues

The greening of festivals

A weekend of music mayhem comes at a price and it's more than the cost of your ticket. The environmental impact of creating a temporary town on greenfield land is shocking in these days of eco-awareness.

The carbon footprint of transporting equipment, stalls and bands, not to mention the mass movement of people travelling to and from the festival site by car, and the traffic chaos that often ensues, can be a major drain on the environment. Add to that onsite electricity, water, waste management and disruption to the land itself, and it's amazing that some festivals still have no environmental policy.

But change is already at hand. While festival audiences have long been receptive to new ideas and environmental concerns, it's not always been easy to put these ideas into practice. The Green Fields at Glastonbury have

been a notable exception, and sustainable eco-festivals like Big Green Gathering, and 2007's 2000 Trees, have made huge efforts to showcase alternative energies and low-impact living. Now nearly all the bigger festivals are keen to establish their green credentials, with commitments by their organizers (if not always by festivalgoers) to be greener.

The environmental organization A Greener Festival works closely with festival managements to work on the key areas where they can make a difference. They share best practices and offer a platform for discussion on improving the green credentials of UK festivals.

Green Futures Festivals, which runs part of Glastonbury, has been chipping away at this for 20 years, and offers consultancy and advice to organizers, as well as a wealth of links and information on its website.

For festival fans, the difference between a really green festival and any other can be subtle, like being asked to sort waste into different containers for recycling, or finding that all the food stalls serve up meals with wooden cutlery rather than plastic (wooden cutlery and plates can be conveniently recycled along with organic food waste).

Some festivals boast of their recycling plans on their official programme, but you might find yourself camping in an outlying field where there's no recycling station set up. Likewise, although main market areas might have separated bins, are they emptied often enough, or will overflowing food debris start blowing in the wind and blighting the area?

Festivals are currently being encouraged by A Greener Festival to organize shuttle buses from local train stations to avoid traffic congestion onsite and reduce carbon emissions associated with travel to the festival. Lift-sharing is a form of more organized hitchhiking and, within safety limits, it's being actively encouraged by Glastonbury and some other festivals as a way of filling those cars that do go to festivals. The Shambala festival makes a £10 charge for cars onsite, putting the income towards providing public transport alternatives.

Did you know that as well as much of Glastonbury Festival being sustainable (powered by the elements, composting toilets, etc.), Worthy Farm is spread with compost made from food waste at the festival?

One growth area for environmental damage at festivals is left-behind tents and camping equipment. Tents have dropped in price so much in recent years, that it can seem not worth the effort of packing up at the end of a full-on weekend, so thousands of tents are left where they stand. While some festivals have arrangements with charities to recycle abandoned tents for the homeless and needy, these still have to be packed properly by the owners before being handed in at a depot in the camping fields. Glastonbury, Reading and Leeds have an arrangement with Give Me Shelter to donate unwanted tents, wellies and sleeping gear to charity.

The good news is that festivals do seem to be taking the environmental, sustainable message to heart. Hopefully in a few years, a book like this will be able to take for granted that festivals are great examples of meeting the environmental challenge head on.

LINKS

A Greener Festival
www.agreenerfestival.com
Event Recycling www.eventrecycling.co.uk
Freewheelers www.freewheelers.com/
Give Me Shelter
www.globalhand.org/givemeshelter
Green Futures Festivals
http://greenfuturesfestivals.org.uk
Liftshare www.liftshare.org
Two Thousand Trees
www.twothousandtreesfestival.co.uk

Handy tips for green campers

- Minimize the amount of packaging on products you buy.
- Avoid buying over-packaged goods and individual portion packs.
- Buy durable products, returnable bottles and containers that can be refilled.
- Look out for recycled goods and those packaged in recycled materials.
- Cut down on packaging by buying your fruit and vegetables loose.
- Buy Fairtrade and organic food, drinks and products at stalls if possible.
- Use re-sealable containers to keep your food fresh (to reduce the amount of plastic film and aluminium foil you throw away).
- Use rechargeable batteries.
- Where you can, recycle what you cannot reuse.
- Don't drop your litter. Use the bins and recycling units!
- Litter-pickers are lovely! Please help them and make up for 'messy' times.
- Car share or use public transport.
- Turn off taps and showers when finished.
- Don't leave rubbish or indeed your entire camping set behind!
- Re-use your carrier bags.
- Take recycling and waste bags to keep you campsite clean and tidy.

Live by the 'LEAVE NO TRACE' philosophy.
(Reproduced by permission of www.agreenerfestival.com)

Festivalgoers with disabilities

Most festivals take great care to accommodate music fans with disabilities offering dedicated camping areas, viewing platforms and disabled toilets.

Disabled camping is usually available to registered disabled people and often those with temporary disabilities such as broken legs. The site is usually a flattish field, with dedicated ramped toilets and sometimes showers, and proximity to the main entertainment areas is usually fairly good. Festival toilets are famously awful and that's why some people see disabled loos as a cleaner, roomier, queue-free alternative – and proceed to turn them into more disaster zones! That's why when you find them, dedicated disabled toilets using the pass-key system are so welcome.

Some festivals, such as V, issue special wristbands for disabled festivalgoers and allow access to viewing ramps. Viewing platforms are sometimes great but can be too far from the action, and may be unstewarded (so anyone can use them) and overcrowded for the biggest acts. You will usually be allowed one friend or helper to join you on the platform.

Attitude is Everything was set up in response to

A disabled steward who works with the disability access organization Attitude is Everything shares one of his fondest festival memories.
Of all the people I've met over the years I would say one of the bravest was at Leeds in 2007. A guy called John from Liverpool turned up on the disabled campsite to ask if there was anyone who could help him. He had travelled from Liverpool by train and shuttle bus to the festival on his own, with just his sleeping bag, so we allowed him to sleep in the information tent. The amazing thing about this is that he is 100 per cent blind. We had stewards and security escorting him between stages and back to the campsite each night and gave the guy a great weekend.
Tony, Hartlepool

USEFUL TIPS

- Plan ahead – contact the festival disability office well in advance to make sure you can get the assistance you need and access to the disabled campsite.
- Most festivals allow you to bring a non-disabled personal assistant at no extra charge. You're going to be popular at sold-out festivals!
- Bring spare batteries for hearing aids.
- Cycling gloves for wheelchair-users can make getting about easier.
- Glastonbury regular Flash Bristow recommends investing in reflective tape and glow sticks to decorate your crutches or wheelchair – you'll look funky and reduce the chances of people falling over you at night.

the complaints from people with disabilities of unfair treatment at music venues, clubs and festivals. The project works positively with the music industry to raise awareness of their obligations under the DDA and was launched in September 2000.

Some 200 'mystery shoppers' – volunteers with disabilities – write up festivals and events from the point of view of attendees with similar disabilities, and these are collated on their website. Attitude is Everything also provide stewards for special areas for those with disabilities at several festivals.

Working with festival organizers, they have seen some positive changes, notably Latitude in 2007, which installed a hearing loop in the comedy, literary and poetry arenas for those customers who use hearing aids. Latitude also offered free British Sign Language and Sign Supported English interpreters for deaf festivalgoers as well as a deaf-blind interpreter on request – great innovations that other festivals may take heed of in future.

LINKS

Attitude is Everything
www.attitudeiseverything.org.uk
Glastonbury on a stick by Flash Bristow
www.gorge.org/glastonbury/onnastick.shtml

for the camp-o-phobics

Hi de hi! Are you one of those for whom festivals sound fun, but you can't face sleeping under canvas, no matter how posh? Compost toilets are fine in theory but you'd never use one?

There is a type of festival designed just for you. Taking over good old British holiday camps, you can join hundreds of like-minded music fans for a weekend of bands, day and night, plus funfair rides, sports facilities and your own private chalet to retire to when it all gets too much.

One of the best known of these weekenders (as they are known) is All Tomorrow's Parties, which pulls together bands from the avant garde and alternative end of the scene. For psychobilly fans, the annual Speedfreaks Ball is a must and, in a similar vein, Concrete Jungle, held at Pontins Camber Sands in East Sussex in 2007, is a punky weekend for all the family. The holiday centres themselves often organize regular themed music weekends, usually starring names from a decade gone by.

See also Festivals Lite pages 74-75

Festivals for free

Once upon a time anyone who wanted to go to a festival without paying could simply jump the fence – if it hadn't been trampled down already. It was almost accepted by festival organizers that there would be a certain percentage of people at the festival who had not paid for their ticket. On occasion, like at the Isle of Wight in 1970, a ticketed festival became a free festival by default due to so many crashing the event.

But as this became an increasing problem, especially at Glastonbury, with well-coordinated gangs running the fence-jumps and charging people for a leg-up the wall, organizers got tough and these days Berlin Wall-style fences keep those without tickets firmly on the wrong side of the party.

But for those in the know, there are plenty of ways to get to a favourite festival for free, if you're prepared to contribute in other ways.

ARTISTS ONLY

The most glamorous way to get to a festival for free is to become a rock star and play there. It's not as unattainable as it sounds. Most festivals offer slots on smaller stages to unsigned bands that send in demos, or are local to the event. In this case, forward planning pays off. Make enquiries for the following year almost as soon as one festival is over, and keep the organizers updated so they

remember your band's name. Most unsigned band slots are filled months ahead of an event. Of course the term artist covers not only bands, but comedians, street performers and cabaret acts. As well as the chance to play to a large crowd, artists usually are given separate camping and a backstage area to hang out in – like real rock stars!

PRESS CALL

Another tried and tested way to get in for free is to become a member of the press. You don't have to be a journalist by trade but the ability to string a well-crafted sentence together helps. Contact your local radio station or free newspaper and offer to write a review focusing on local people at the festival and bands from the area. The editor may agree to let you apply for a press pass using their name.

As you would expect, press passes for Glastonbury and Reading are notoriously hard to come by – if you are looking to kick-start a music journalism career, aim for accreditation to the smaller festivals and build the contacts to work your way up over a couple of years. Press tickets usually allow you access to a hospitality area 'backstage' and possibly a chance to interview some of the bands performing. But if you're clearly there for a freebie and not attempting to work, you're unlikely to be asked back the following year.

FESTIVAL CREW

If you can't play and you can't write, there are lots of other ways to work your ticket at a festival. Stewarding, security, bar work, information, recycling and welfare all employ staff. You can forget contacting the big festivals like Glastonbury direct, as nearly all the jobs are contracted out to the various organizations and companies who specialize in just these roles. It is always worth contacting smaller festivals well ahead of time to see if they need any general helping hands – see their websites for details.

The main difference between paid work at a festival and volunteer work (apart from the money!) is that volunteers tend to work shorter shifts and have more time to enjoy the festival experience. But even if you are given a place as a volunteer you will be expected to work your full hours – you may be asked to pay a large deposit (returnable after the festival) to ensure you don't just do a runner once you're inside. The minimum age for just about every type of work is 18.

BAR WORK

Beer tent operators range from the local pub to big breweries to, at many of the biggest events, the Workers Beer Company. First find out who is running the beer tents and contact them, letting them know about your bar experience and availability to work.

If you are a member of a trade union, the Workers Beer Company could be your route to Glastonbury, Reading and Leeds, and many smaller festivals. The company was set up to raise funds for left-leaning organizations, and employs self-organizing teams from union branches and pressure groups. Each team-member is paid a reasonable hourly rate which goes to the organization, not the individual.

Bar work is, depending on the shift and the location of the tent, anything from laid back and fun to intense and thankless. The bar staff get their own campsite with showers and security, meal tokens and enough time off to enjoy some of the festival. Competition between organizations is fierce for the plum jobs like Glastonbury and Reading, and there is often a long waiting list to find a place on a team.

STEWARDING

Oxfam has built a reputation as the main force in volunteer stewarding, and again stewards are given free entry and secure camping in return for several shifts of hard work. Oxfam trains stewards, who can be called upon to undertake many different roles including assisting the public, checking tickets, parking control, dealing with lost kids – and generally making sure the event runs smoothly.

Stewards have to be reasonably fit and have to stay sober during their long shifts, which may involve standing on one spot for hours at a time, miles from the action.

LITTER-PICKING AND RECYCLING

These are jobs you can contact Glastonbury directly about. Alternatively, there are paid jobs through some festival contractors.

The Green Police are a bunch of volunteers who try to make recycling fun. They dress up in outrageous costumes and wander about festivals encouraging people to be tidy, clean and green in a happy, playful and humorous way. It helps to be an extrovert and a natural performer as lots of people want their photos taken with Green Police.

FESTIVAL WELFARE

Everyone from The Salvation Army, Samaritans, The Wellfairies and Reading Festival Point are at various festivals to make sure people have a good time – and if they're not, they provide someone to talk to and help with crash spaces, blankets and just someone to talk to. If you have experience of counselling and you would like to help people who are having a tough time amid the festivities, contact an organization to see how you can help.

LINKS

VOLUNTEERING

Festival Medical Services Ltd
www.festivalmedical.co.uk

Festival Samaritans
www.festivalsamaritans.org

Green Police
http://savetheworldclub.org/greenpolice.htm

Oxfam stewarding
www.oxfam.org.uk/get_involved/stewarding/index.html

Reading Festival Point
www.readingwelfarepoint.org.uk

Workers Beer Company
www.workersbeer.org.uk

PAID WORK

Cash and Traffic Management
www.cashandtrafficmanagement.com

DC Site Services – recycling, litter, stewarding, traffic management
www.dcsiteservices.com/calendar

Free lifts
www.liftshare.org

LOCAL ORGANIZATIONS

If you live locally to a festival and are involved in a local charity or non-profit organization, there may be opportunities to contribute to the festival in some way. Make sure you put your ideas directly to the festival management in plenty of time.

NATIONAL CHARITIES AND ORGANIZATIONS

Many festivals have stalls run by charities and pressure groups, such as Water Aid or Amnesty International or the Samaritans. If you are a supporter of these charities, you can apply through them to work.

MEDICAL STAFF

Qualified medical staff (not students) can volunteer for most festivals through Festival Medical Services Ltd, which started back in the early days of Glastonbury and provides medical centres on site. FMS is a registered charity and raises funds for other medical and environmental charities.

St John's Ambulance volunteers are also a fixture offering first aid at many festivals.

TRADERS

Sometimes if a festival is sold out, a group of you can still trade there for little more than the cost of a few tickets – plus you have the opportunity to make your money back. Most traders recruit staff from their friends, but if you talk to traders early in the season and they like the look of you, you might find yourself called upon to help out later that year. To book a stall, contact each festival directly through their website.

family friendly

Mention to a colleague or your family that you are taking young children to a festival and you should be prepared for shock and horror. If your colleague's idea of festivals hasn't moved on from the lawless, amenity-free seventies, then this is understandable. But thankfully today's festival organizers are wise to the value of the family market, and lay on lots of extras for the little ones, as well as letting them in free or for a token price.

If you've got children but love going to gigs, festivals can provide a lifeline for the babysitter-challenged. Dozens of great bands, mainly in the open air, and the kids can come along too. Great – in theory.

The truth is, a festivalgoing experience with kids will be a very different one from your days as a singleton or couple. In fact, when comparing notes afterwards with childless friends, you may wonder whether they've been to a different festival – one with fetish trapeze artists, brilliant 2 a.m. comedy and a secret disco. On the other hand, those without small accomplices have no reason to enter the bouncy castle, join the puppet workshop or attend a fairy party.

Bringing babies means either taking childcare shifts with your other half to let you watch your must-see bands, or standing a long way back so that they won't complain it's too loud or be crushed in a mosh pit.

It means listening to the sounds of your favourite headline artist across three fields as you change nappies in a torchlit tent. It means waking up at 7 a.m. on Sunday morning to high-pitched demands for breakfast, when you only crashed out at 5 a.m. And it means spending the afternoon in a brightly coloured tent making hand puppets with toddlers while your mates are drinking the beer tent dry.

Put off yet? No? Great, because although it may not be the hell-raising experience of your pre-parenting days, it's still a lot of fun.

Not every event is great for small children though – apart from Glastonbury none of the biggest festivals specifically cater for children, and they tend to attract a fairly raucous crowd, which makes them far from kid-friendly. Even Glastonbury,

with its immense size, is a logistical nightmare when you're looking after a brood of small people. The surge of people leaving the main stage can be quite terrifying when you're only half the height of everyone else.

Kids' provision at most festivals ensures your offspring will make new friends, enjoy some new experiences and almost certainly have a much better time than if they had stayed at home.

There's the novelty of camping, for a start. Family camping zones are usually close to play areas, and are patrolled at night for noisy parties but are tolerant of crying babies.

Children's zones range from absolutely nothing at the big, corporate festivals (Reading, V and T), via homespun play areas, to fantastic, secure children's activity and entertainment areas (Guilfest's is like a self-contained mini-festival in its own right).

Organizers can't stress enough, though, that kids' areas aren't crèches – you are expected to supervise your children while they play. Bestival is a notable exception to this; you can book your children into the official crèche and pop off to enjoy some bands.

Kids' areas tend to be open during daylight hours only, and often wind down on the final day of a festival. If you're planning on taking the children out with you to see headline acts, make sure they have somewhere cosy to sleep – be it a buggy, shelter, or groundsheet and blankets.

As your children get older, it gets easier and more fun for the parents. More and more festivals (such as Beautiful Days) have areas specifically for young teenagers and older children with lots of activities aimed at their tastes – and you really can leave them entertained in safety for a couple of hours. One of the best performances at Beautiful Days is the fire show put on by older children who have learned to fire juggle over the weekend – not as dangerous as it sounds!

When did you start taking your children to festivals?
My partner and I were festival fans but after our baby was born we didn't know if it would be the right thing to do to take her along. Eventually we took Lizzie to the Isle of Wight when she was a year old, with a buggy and about a million wet wipes. She loved it, although we didn't get to see too many bands!
Sarah, West Midlands

Tips for happy kids

- Bring layers of clothes – plenty of them – but nothing white!
- A few favourite toys will ensure harmony.
- Budget for a few new toys bought at the festival – there are always crazes amongst the kids, from light sabres and bubble swords to glow sticks. Keep the peace by buying cheap treats.
- Peltor ear defenders for kids are the latest festival must-have, as popularized by Gwynnie and Chris's little'uns on a Coldplay tour. Buy them for around £10 a pair on the internet and watch your favourite bands without risking their hearing.
- Really cheap buggies are brilliant as kids tire easily and suddenly at festivals. It's also somewhere to carry your stuff.
- If your kids are too old for pushchairs they will still crash out when you least expect it. Wheelbarrows lined with blankets, Radio Flyer red wagons and top-of-the-range Chariot child transporters are all common solutions.
- Take plenty of packaged food – such as small packs of biscuits and crackers, bananas, individual water bottles – for instant fixes and to beat food queues.
- Wet wipes are an absolute festival essential with or without kids, but with kids take as many as you can possibly manage. You won't regret it!
- Disposable nappies for babies are pretty much essential for all but the most hardcore green parents. Biodegradable nappies are available in supermarkets and baby shops – look out for Moltex and Nature Boy & Girl brands. Even if your child is usually dry at night, pyjama pants are a good fall-back to avoid unexpected wet sleeping bags.
- A potty – preferably with a lid – will save the discomfort and horror of nocturnal trips to festival loos.
- Use a marker pen or henna to write your mobile number on your child's arm in case you get separated.
- Point out stewards in tabards as the sort of people your child should make for if he or she becomes lost.

festival style

Kate Moss has a lot to answer for. By making regular appearances in *Heat* and the tabloid gossip pages, posing backstage at Glastonbury or V with a pint in her AAA-wristbanded hand, while looking divine in designer heels, micro-mini and flouncy scarves, she has single-handedly invented festival chic.

Moss has inspired thousands of impressionable and fashion-conscious women to pack their Alexander McQueen skull scarves, suede boots and velvet hats and visit a festival for the first time.

NEVER FOR THE SECOND TIME

The sharp shock of the general population areas of any festival underline the class differences between everyday wristbands and those with access to the hospitality areas. The mud for one thing. Backstage, even in bad weather, you'll find most areas carpeted, or at least covered in a layer of dry straw. Celebrities may never venture out of this elite area. Chances are they will be helicopered on and off site, sleep in a country house hotel and not even consider trying the same festival food as everyone else.

Kate Moss: style icon for young women across the country

The trick to looking good at a festival is to not worry what you look like. Put comfort first and you can't go wrong. Once the basics are in place then by all means chuck on the Alexander McQueen scarf – just leave the Louboutins at home.

WHAT ARE THE CLOTHING ESSENTIALS?

Let's start with the feet. Nothing kills the festival spirit quicker than cold, damp feet. Waterproof hiking boots with gripping soles can work in all but the wettest weather – but are no substitute for wellingtons in a mud bath.

WELLIES. Pretty much essential – cheap, colourful as you like and a cinch to put on and take off. Just remember to wear an extra pair of socks – not only because they are nice and toasty but it's surprisingly easy to have wellies sucked off your feet in mud puddles if they are too loose. Alternatively, for really fine weather, open sandals can be lovely, but forget fashion sandals, crocs, even trainers unless you come by Winnebago – they don't pass the practical test.

Dame Shirley Bassey dons suitable footwear at Glastonbury

SOCKS. Please not with sandals, but you're going to need them the rest of the time - possibly even while you sleep. Take enough for each day you're away, then double it. Sometimes you might need two pairs and even wellies can let the wet in sometimes.

UNDERWEAR. For goodness sake, bring a change for every day. You're unlikely to be having a daily shower, so the small comfort of clean socks and pants can make you feel fresher. And don't forget the spares.

SKIRTS. Some women insist on wearing skirts to festivals. Are they perhaps trying to smuggle a ticketless friend in underneath? Or booze?

TROUSERS. Combats or jeans and a pair of cut-offs for hot daytimes. Just make sure they have lots of pockets, deep and zipped, for your cash, tickets, phone, tissues and wet wipes.

TOPS. Tiny vest tops are great for hot weather (provided you remember the sunscreen) and fold up small in your rucksack. Take several. Emulating Kate Moss is one thing, but if you spill curry sauce down your only T-shirt on the Friday night you're going to look more like Rab C. Nesbitt for the rest of the weekend. Official festival T-shirts usually cost a small fortune but make great souvenirs and tend to be good quality.

After the sun goes down you can't beat a good old festival jumper – something that comes down past your bum, with sleeves long enough to hide your hands in. Fleeces are a good alternative – the bonus is they will dry quickly if they get wet.

Packaway kagoules and macs are great for wet festivals – they keep you dry without making you too hot and fold away when not in use.

HATS of any description are a festival essential. Choose a style with a brim to keep the sun or rain off your face. In fact, buy your hat at the festival, the choice is always great and prices are low.

SUNGLASSES. Another essential. Take a cheapish pair as arenas are always littered with broken, trampled shades.

SWING YOUR PANTS IN FANCY DRESS

OK, so you're not going to try to look like a fashion icon this weekend. You've got the practical gear all sorted. But the chances are that by Saturday night, you'll think it's a great idea to look like a fairy. Or a pirate. Or a showgirl. Yes, festivals have gone fancy dress.

There have always been colourful characters at festivals – clowns, street performers, Björk – but a few years ago, some forum users came up with the idea of dressing up on (usually) the Saturday night, sometimes to a theme, sometimes in ridiculous costumes.

Soon the festival organizers themselves started sanctioning the idea and before long fancy dress became the norm on an agreed night at some festivals. Others, notably Bestival, are pretty much fancy dress all the time.

If you want to dress fancy, the secret is to do so in harmony with the aforementioned festival clothing principles. Work with the weather. A fuchsia wig and tiara could make you glad of the protection the polyfibre hairs can offer against a biting wind – less glad on a very hot afternoon.

If the festival looks like being muddy, choose a look that won't be ruined by a bit of splatter. Fred and Wilma Flintstone are good. Pirates usually look no worse for a layer of filth. The Dying Swan from Swan Lake? Not so good, unless the costume has thigh-length white angler's waders.

If you find planning a costume a bit out of your league, improvise. You can pick up accessories from many of the festival market stalls and, with a bit of imagination, you can pass as a vicar, sheikh, witch or superhero easily enough. Or you can go the whole hog and hire an outfit. Some festivals have specialist outfitters who rent you amazing costumes.

One great thing about fancy dress is it helps people create a festival personality and leave behind their everyday selves, which is after all what the festival vibe is all about.

festival food

Festivals offer everything from full English breakfasts and afternoon tea to exotic feasts from Morocco, the Far East and quite possibly, other solar systems.

Catering options span the comfortably familiar to the wildly adventurous – far broader in range than the sort of restaurants you'd find on any average high street. Many are organic and free range, while vegetarians and vegans are always well-catered for.

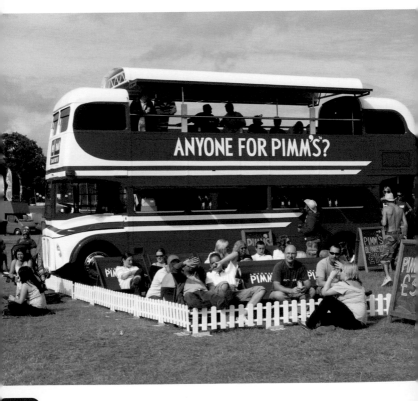

FOOD TO TAKE TO FESTIVALS

- Big blocks of chocolate (plain doesn't melt as much).
- Energy and breakfast bars.
- Bags of posh crisps and jars of salsa.
- Bananas, not too ripe.
- Apples.
- Hard cheese. Nothing soft or too smelly.
- Oatcakes or crackers.
- Cheap biscuits such as bourbons for late-night munchies.
- If you must carry tins, go for the ring-pull lid type. Sweetcorn straight from the tin is less disgusting or messy than cold baked beans.
- Variety packs of breakfast cereal eaten straight from the pack – without milk!
- Packets of mixed nuts, seeds and raisins.
- And don't forget chewing gum for instantly freshening your hangover mouth.

Whatever time of the day or night you're awake, you can bet there's a food stall not far away ready to serve you some hot food. From hot tea and toast at 7 a.m. for harassed parents and lively children, to 5 a.m. Irish coffees and pancakes for the rave crew – festival catering achieves a level of customer service and availability almost unknown in everyday life.

Don't expect cheap eats – you'll be paying around £5 per dish, and quite a lot more if you go for one of the Full Monty specials so beloved of hungry and hungover fans. Fresh juice or coffee will set you back another £2–£3 and cold soft drinks in a can are about £1 a time, but rare as hen's teeth in hot weather.

Most stalls are takeaways, but you may find a table in a café tent or, even better, in an afternoon tea marquee, staffed by burlesque performers (Bestival!).

At most festivals traders have to agree to use eco-friendly recyclable plates and cutlery; unfortunately this doesn't have much effect on the amount of litter discarded around the food market areas.

DIY FOOD

You can save quite a lot of cash and beat the queues by bringing your own food, at least for some of the weekend's meals or snacks. You don't need an actual cooker – we're talking simple sandwiches and light bites.

Festival fodder

If you're lucky enough to have a cooker of some description, you can cook up a great meal with one gas ring. You don't get extra points at a festival for cooking from scratch; you have too many things to see. Fast and convenient is the way to go.

Here are two favourites: Note that the washing up for both these dishes is minimal – one saucepan and one fork. If you've ever tried washing up at a festival water point, in cold water, while standing in a bog, you'll understand why.

FESTIVAL PASTA

Takes 10 minutes from packet to plate. Requires a camp stove with one burner. One saucepan. Fork.

Ingredients

• Enough dried pasta for one or two people
• Packet pasta sauce such as Dolmio Express
• Hard cheese, chopped

Boil water and add the pasta, cook for prescribed time, and drain.

Add sauce to drained hot pasta and mix.

Immediately, add chopped pieces of cheese, which will melt in hot pasta.

Eat with fork from saucepan.

BEAN BIRYANI

Even quicker; takes about five minutes, tops.

Ingredients

• Pack of Uncle Ben's microwave pilau rice (or similar)
• Tin of beans (curried is best)

Cook rice in a little boiling water for a few minutes, while stirring constantly.

Add beans and mix in well while keeping pan on a low heat.

Eat with fork from saucepan.

Can you feel the magic?

Some little touches make the difference between a concert and a festival.

HEALING

Whether there's a whole healing field or just a few tents, alternative practitioners and festivals go hand-in-hand. If you've never tried reiki, crystal healing, chanting, yoga, homeopathy or chakra balancing, now is your opportunity. If you overdo the partying one night, there will be someone with healing hands ready to put you back together the next day, for a small price. Have you tried rock 'n' rain? It's not a new type of music, just a therapy combining essential oils, massage and gentle rocking movements – perfect after too much rock 'n' roll. Some healers work on donation only, others will charge up to £20 for a treatment.

FORTUNE-TELLING

Could this weekend be the start of a new chapter in your life? Many apparently think so – tarot readers, clairvoyants, palmists, pendulum-swingers, tea-leaf readers and even more esoteric purveyors of fortune-telling are all available to set you on your new path. Strangely, not many readers have dedicated stalls – you will often find fortune-tellers sharing a space with a retailer, or simply setting out an unofficial area on a rug near a footpath. Prices range from about £5 for a quick taster reading to £20 for an in-depth session.

SPIRITUALITY

For many people, the most spiritual experience they are likely to have at a festival is being part of thousands of out-of-tune voices singing along to the headline act's biggest chorus. But for others, the shared experience of a festival is an ideal time for bonding with like-minded souls and searching for greater meaning in life.

Spiritual and religious groups are often evident at festivals, hoping to tap into the mood. The Hare Krishnas are a broke festival fan's dream – their free vegetarian food draws the crowds, and plenty stay for the chanting and meditation afterwards. Other religions – Christian, Buddhist, Pagan, whatever – get in on the act with free coffee and chats about God, holy massages, feet washing, or just quiet spaces where you can relax and find yourself among the chaos. On a more personal level, pockets of spirituality open up wherever you look for it – Glastonbury's King's Meadow at dawn, in the dying embers of a campfire, in the jangle of the temple balls you bought in the market.

PUBLIC ART

Unique expressions of creativity make sense in the context of a festival, like The Wishing Tree. This UV-lit community artwork evolves with each outing and literally carries the hopes and wishes of thousands of festival folk.

World-renowned willow artist Serena De La Hey has supplied Glastonbury and other festivals with large-scale organic sculptures of stretching figures.

The Mutoid Waste Company, a group of sci-fi influenced kinetic artists, weld together scrap metal to make the most jaw-dropping moving metal monsters, complete with smoke and lights that find their way through an unsuspecting festival crowd.

LINKS

Serena de la Hey
www.serenadelahey.com
Wishing Tree
www.wishingtree.co.uk

Dance arenas

No proper festival these days goes without a dance arena, even if otherwise it's wall-to-wall rock music.

Dance tents and arenas have grown massively in popularity, drawing in world-class club DJs, with top musicians from main stage bands blagging guest DJ spots, to Ibiza corporate sponsors keen to get in on the act.

The party vibe in a dance arena often runs late into the night and, if you wander in from the main stage, it can seem as if you've walked into a different festival. The glow stick brigade can keep things going long after the other stages have closed down. From dub reggae to techno and live bands making unannounced appearances, dance tents are a little bit of the Ibiza vibe in a British field and add an extra dimension to a festival.

SOME OF THE BEST DANCE TENTS/ARENAS

Bacardi B-Live – Southport Weekender, Isle of Wight Festival, T in the Park, Oxegen, V Festival
Bedrock International – SW4
Dance East – Glastonbury Festival
Duracell Powerhouse – T in the Park, Leeds Festival, Download, Connect
M8 Present: Cream & Goodgrief – Creamfields
Polysexual Terrace – Global Gathering
Rizla Invisible Players Arena – Lovebox, Bestival
Samsung Big Top – Bestival
Slam Tent – T in the Park
Strongbow Cider House – Isle of Wight Festival, Global Gathering, V Festival, Creamfields
The Clash Arena – Rock Ness

Courtesy of Virtual Festivals

festival songs

Although certain tracks can capture the mood of a
festival – think Jimi Hendrix's *Star Spangled Banner*
at Woodstock, Pulp's *Common People* at Glastonbury
1995 – fewer songs are actually written about festivals.
Here are a few classic gems and forgotten turkeys
for your festival iPod.

'STINKING UP THE GREAT OUTDOORS' – SPINAL TAP
(from *Break Like the Wind*, 2004)
> *Late afternoon in the open air;*
> *A human sea made out of mud and hair.*
> *Ain't nothing like a festival crowd:*
> *There's too many people so we play too loud.*

Possibly the most honest festival song ever, the spoof supergroup's ode to
festivals, mud and alcohol from their comeback album will strike a chord
with anyone who attended a weather-hit festival in 2007.

'MUSHROOM FESTIVAL IN HELL' – WEEN
(from *God WEEN Satan – The Oneness*, 1990)
> *The wind is howling and the time is right for fear*
> *In the emergence in the phosphorescent tears*
> *And all the hippies gonna lick the mind of god?*
> *They've already been immersed in the wad.*

Wacky Pennsylvania underground duo Ween experience the dark side of
festival life, surrounded by tripping hippies in this early track.

'WOODSTOCK' – JONI MITCHELL
(from *Ladies of the Canyon*, 1970)
> *By the time we got to Woodstock*
> *We were half a million strong*
> *And everywhere there was song and celebration.*

This first-hand account of the legendary festival is a flower-power classic and has been covered both by Matthew's Southern Comfort and Crosby, Stills, Nash and Young – despite the fact that its author was far from Woodstock at the time. Joni Mitchell had turned down the chance to perform in favour of making a television appearance at the event. Although she has had a very successful career, Mitchell has since said that missing Woodstock was one of the biggest regrets of her life.

'GLASTONBURY REVISITED' – COSMIC ROUGH RIDERS
(from *Enjoy the Melodic Sunshine*, 2000)

> *Glastonbury's golden sun*
> *Will shine its love on everyone*
> *Where have all the angels gone*
> *Now that all the acid's done.*

The Glasgow neo-psychedelics' most obvious track on an album that belongs on every festival sound system. The story of a visit to Pilton's famous festival, involving drugs, sex and a visitation by angels.

'FESTIVAL SONG' – GOOD CHARLOTTE
(from self-titled debut album, 2001)

> *I don't want your boring life.*
> *And I don't want your 9 to 5.*
> *Or anyone to tell me how to live my life.*

The pop punkers' appearance at Maryland's HFStival in 2001 was a breakthrough moment for the MTV-friendly band. The song celebrates the feeling of freedom a festival can give fans – and the video for the single was filmed during the band's set at the festival.

'BATTLE OF THE BEANFIELD' – THE LEVELLERS
(from *Levelling the Land*, 1991)

> *Hey, hey, now can't you see*
> *There's nothing here that you can call free*
> *They're getting their kicks*
> *They're laughing at you and me.*

Downbeat and angry, this eyewitness account of the police raid on travellers at the 1985 Stonehenge gathering is still a classic in festival stalwarts The Levellers' set.

'THE MEMORY OF A FREE FESTIVAL' – DAVID BOWIE

(from *Space Oddity*, 1970)

> *The children of the summer's end*
> *Gathered in the dampened grass*
> *We played our songs and felt the London sky*
> *Resting on our hands*
> *It was God's land*
> *It was ragged and naive*
> *It was heaven.*

Bowie's homage to a South London free festival held in Croydon in 1969 was released as a single on both sides of the Atlantic, but was a resounding flop. The Bowie magic that has since headlined classic Glastonbury and Isle of Wight festivals wasn't quite together yet, it seems.

'WOODSTOCK FESTIVAL' – JIMI HENDRIX

(poem inspired by Hendrix's legendary Woodstock appearance, 1969)

> *500,000 halos ...*
> *Outshined the mud and history.*
> *We washed and drank in*
> *God's tears of joy,*
> *And for once ... and for everyone ...*
> *The truth was not a mystery.*

Contrary to the image of Woodstock and the lyrics presented here, it wasn't all about an ego-free communal love-in experience. Hendrix had insisted on closing the festival, as he wanted to headline the event. That meant his blistering set didn't materialize until Monday morning – after all but 60,000 of the half-million music fans had gone home.